OXFORD
INDIA SHORT
INTRODUCTIONS

THE PARTITION OF INDIA

The Oxford India Short
Introductions are concise,
stimulating, and accessible guides
to different aspects of India.
Combining authoritative analysis,
new ideas, and diverse perspectives,
they discuss subjects which are
topical yet enduring, as also
emerging areas of study and debate.

OTHER TITLES IN THE SERIES

For more information, visit our website:
https://india.oup.com/content/series/o/
oxford-india-short-introductions/

OXFORD
INDIA SHORT
INTRODUCTIONS

THE PARTITION
OF INDIA

HAIMANTI ROY

OXFORD
UNIVERSITY PRESS

OXFORD
UNIVERSITY PRESS

Oxford University Press is a department of the University of Oxford.
It furthers the University's objective of excellence in research, scholarship,
and education by publishing worldwide. Oxford is a registered trademark of
Oxford University Press in the UK and in certain other countries.

Published in India by
Oxford University Press
2/11 Ground Floor, Ansari Road, Daryaganj, New Delhi 110 002, India

ISBN-13 (print edition): 978-0-19-948869-8
ISBN-10 (print edition): 0-19-948869-X

ISBN-13 (eBook): 978-0-19-909382-3
ISBN-10 (eBook): 0-19-909382-2

Typeset in 11/14.3 Bembo Std
by The Graphics Solution, New Delhi 110 092
Printed in India by Replika Press Pvt. Ltd

For
Rahul and Karna

Contents

Preface and Acknowledgements

In a recent survey published in the spring of 2017, the Pew Research Center, a well-known US-based think tank, noted that 72 per cent of Indians view their neighbour Pakistan unfavourably. Their survey seems credible as one reads the news or interacts with middle-class Indians in segregated social spaces. As I write this, there is an alarming rise in violence and intolerance in India, especially against minority Muslims and Christians. They have been targets of vigilante lynch mobs seeking to 'save cows', seen by many Hindus as holy. In addition to being perceived as 'beef-eaters' and 'cow-killers', Indian minorities are also demonized as Pakistani and Western loyalists. The 1947 division remains front and centre as questions of national belonging and citizenship periodically resurface, and the postmemory of India and Pakistan rethink their relationship in oppositional terms rather than emphasizing commonalities.

It would be easy to see the Partition of India as the symbolic culmination of age-old animus between Hindus, Muslims, and Sikhs, a 'clash of civilizations' that has continued to fester through issues of border skirmishes, water wars, the global and regional wars on terrorism, and, of course, Kashmir. However, I suggest that to do so, to seek answers for the Partition of India within a linear trajectory of communal antagonism, would be to miss the non-linear and multiple paths that brought us to 1947. It would then erase the narratives of plurality, communal unity, and of human connections that dotted those very paths.

This book provides a very brief history of the Partition of India not as a singular event that marked the failure of high politics, but as a messy, long-drawn-out process that was not inevitable. It is no easy task to provide a comprehensive narrative of the Partition within the requirements of this short introduction and to do justice to the rapidly expanding scholarship on the event. However, this book is informed by both recent and initial scholarship on various aspects of why and how the Partition happened, and seeks to acquaint the reader with the human experience of the division as well as its long-term legacies. It attempts to focus on both the Bengal and the Punjab experience and compare and examine why regional experiences were so distinct. Although the Partition directly impacted three new nation states—India, Pakistan, and, later, Bangladesh—this book focuses primarily on its legacies in India.

The book suggests that there is no singular paradigm when one examines the causes of Partition and the experiences of dislocation, rehabilitation migration, and violence in the partitioned regions. Rather, it urges its readers to pay attention to contextual politics, go beyond cultural explanations, and to think about the diverse range of experiences mediated by class, gender, caste, religion, and language. The aim is to introduce and encourage the reader to go further in depth in their quest for knowledge—in this, the book is a guide, a starting point to understanding a fascinating and multifaceted event.

The writing of this book has been a difficult journey, because of the complex subject which needed compression without losing its comprehensive focus and owing to the time I could afford to its writing amidst teaching a 3-3 load at the University of Dayton, USA. I am thus thankful to the Dean of the College of Arts and Sciences for giving me two course releases at the initial stages of the project. I am grateful to my colleagues and friends here, Chris Agnew, Dorian

Borbonus, Una Cadegan, Simanti Dasgupta, Ellen Fleischman, Caroline Merithew, and Juan Santamarina, for their unwavering support and encouragement at various stages of the project. I am grateful for the warm support I have received over the years from Douglas Haynes, Wendy Singer, and Barbara Ramusack.

I have benefitted from my engagement with scholars and students at two conferences— 'Partition in Bengal: Looking Back after 70 Years', organized by Sekhar Bandyopadhyay, Jayanta Sengupta, and Rituparna Roy in August 2017, and 'Partition and Pluralism', at Columbia University, USA, in January 2018. The ideas presented at these conferences by scholars and students have helped immensely in revising the draft manuscript. I would like to thank Paula Braley for the initial round of copyediting. I am grateful to the team at Oxford University Press for their patience and steady encouragement with the project.

My friends inspire me with how they deal with life and in sharing their thoughts and ideas with me. A big thank you to Anuradha Agarwal, Subhra Bhattacharya, Varuni Bhatia, Arvind Elangovan, Sayata Ghose, Sharatee Ghosh, Madhubanti Mukherjeee, Neeti Nair, Alita Nandi, Raisur Rahman, Sudipa Topedar, Sharmadip Basu, and Aparna Vaidik for reminding me of the serious and not-so-serious aspects of our lives. My parents, Haripada Roy and Gouri Roy, did not let their unconditional love for me prevent them from asking, quite often, about the possibility of seeing this book at the next *boi mela* (book fair). Finally, they will get their wish. To Rahul and Karna, more is owed than I can say.

Note on Terminology

Historically accurate names of places have been used wherever applicable. Thus, I have used the old names for cities such as Calcutta, Bombay, and Madras to depict Kolkata, Mumbai, and Chennai. After 1947, East Bengal formally changes its name to East Pakistan in 1956. I have used East Pakistan and East Bengal interchangeably to reflect the particular geographical region and in keeping with how this region was referred to at the time.

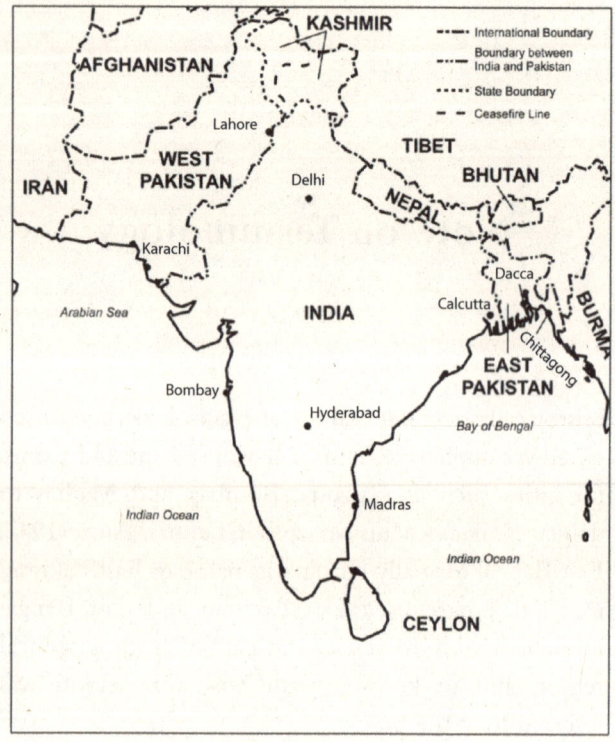

Figure I.1　India Pakistan Overview 1947

Source: Author (Drawn by Robert Booth).
Note: This map does not represent the authentic international boundaries of India. This map is not to scale and is provided for illustrative purposes only.

Introduction
Three Partitions

August 1947 ushered in historical realities that would continue to impact the history of the South Asian subcontinent for years to come. Two new nation states, India and a divided Pakistan, emerged out of the political partition and the British formally quit their jewel in the crown. Punjab and Bengal, two provinces with majority Muslim populations, were divided along religious lines: West Punjab and East Bengal going to Pakistan and East Punjab and West Bengal remaining in India. Pakistan received a larger share of the erstwhile Punjab and Bengal provinces, both of which would have distinct futures. In the subsequent decades, West Punjab became the epicentre of the nation state of Pakistan while East Bengal/Pakistan broke away in 1971 to form the new nation state of Bangladesh.

In effect, there were three simultaneous partitions: of British India, of the province of Bengal, and of the province of Punjab; and their political and socio-economic experiences differed depending on where and on whom one focuses one's investigative lens. An alternative way to think about the three partitions is to think of them conceptually, as three different moments that are part of the same event (Pandey 2001). Either framework, and this book follows the first, suggests that the Partition and its history, memories, and legacies need to move away from a singular narrative to accommodate multiplicities in experiences and divergent political trajectories.

The act of dividing and untangling two nations was undertaken within six short months and involved high-level political decisions. British officials in conjunction with the leaders of the All India National Congress (hereinafter the Congress) and the All India Muslim League (hereinafter the League) met behind closed doors to decide the new international borders, the allocation of financial resources, and the division of the armed forces, civil servants, and bureaucratic departments. In fact, the past itself was to be partitioned, as museums and their collections, archives, and records were divided between the two nations.

The concurrent processes of division, independence, and decolonization engendered the largest forced migrations in the history of the twentieth century. Between 1946 and 1965, nearly nine million Hindus and Sikhs moved to India and approximately five million Muslims moved to both parts of Pakistan. The resulting massive displacement made refugee rehabilitation one of the primary agendas in the post-1947 restructuring of India and Pakistan.

The immediate impact of the Partition was felt in the incomprehensible violence that began with the riots in Calcutta in August 1946 and then spread to Punjab in March 1947. As the violence continued to rage in the immediate aftermath of 1947, it targeted women as symbols of their families, communities, and nations (Butalia 1998). The death toll remains disputed to this day, with figures ranging from 200,000 to 1 million. More than 100,000 women were abducted on both sides of the border (Menon and Bhasin 1998). The experience of violence and migration differed in the north and the east: Punjab and northern India witnessed mass violence and a swift displacement of their populations while Bengal and eastern India underwent smaller scale routine violence and saw chronic migration patterns that lasted until 1971 when the independence of Bangladesh impacted this region differently.

However, even two months before August 1947, there was hardly anyone who could surely predict such a horrific future marked by displacement, insecurity, and trauma. That the British would leave India was a certainty in the general mind, but how and when was up for debate. While the run-up to the Partition had been paved with the rhetoric of anti-colonial nationalism and the two-nation theory, also in existence were other ideas of how independence could be achieved depending on location (Roy 2009; Nair 2011).

Then why did it happen? How did the partition of British India become the only solution in 1947 agreed upon by the British, the Congress, and the League? How and why did regional leaders in Bengal and Punjab support the move to divide their provinces in spite of the inevitable issues of uprooting that would arise? Were there any alternatives to the Partition? Most importantly, was the Partition inevitable?

This book addresses these questions to show how processes at the national, regional, and popular levels converged and diverged to pave the road for the division of India. Further, it focuses on the experiences of violence, uprooting, and divided families that impacted common people during and after 1947. Through a discussion of such processes and the associated memories and experiences, interspersed as they are with silences, the book places the history of the Partition within the broader histories of the post-colonial state.

Scholars have long debated the causes of and the responsibility for the Partition. Many writers persuasively blame the British for the gradual erosion of interwoven community identities and shared traditions. They point out how long-term British efforts to define India as a set of 'distinct communities' based on religion and to imbue such identities with political significance led to Indians self-identifying within such categories (Spear 1958; Singh 1987; Shaikh 1989). Recent assessments, however, argue for shorter, largely contingent, developments in the 1930s and 1940s as the primary reason for the Partition (Chatterji 1994; Jaffrelot 1996; Nair 2011).

The imperatives of nationalist historiographies often influenced different readings of the events and the apportioning of the blame. Thus, in their focus on the tense political and constitutional negotiations between the British and the major Indian political parties, the Congress and the League, and the actions of leading political figures such as Nehru, Jinnah, and Patel, scholars have been haunted by a communal–national binary (Jalal 1998). Such a binary posits Muslim communalism as the antithesis of Indian nationalism, which inevitably led to the Partition.

The argument for age-old communal differences is also useful to explain why Pakistan was necessary. The received wisdom on the creation of Pakistan has been

5

twofold. First, responsibility is attributed to Mohammed Ali Jinnah and the League as representatives of the community in British India, who used the concept of Pakistan as a bargaining chip to ensure better political terms against the Hindu majority in a post-colonial undivided India (Jalal 1985). In this understanding, Jinnah was not really seeking a separate sovereign Pakistan, and the fact that India was partitioned was the consequence of the failure of political negotiations with the Congress. Recent scholarship, seeking to overturn this argument, suggests that a sovereign Pakistan was not only central to Jinnah's ideas but he was also supported by sections of the *ulema* (Islamic religious scholar) in the United Provinces (UP) where the idea of Pakistan found the greatest initial support (Dhulipala 2014).

Second, the narrative incorporates causality in terms of long-term trends and trajectories of minority politics that purportedly gave rise to Muslim communalism and the two-nation theory (Hardy 1972). The demand and support for a separate homeland in the late 1930s made the Partition inevitable. However, as recent scholarship has shown, rather than intransigent political and religious ideas and identities inexorably moving towards a final denouement, contemporary leaders in Bengal and Punjab continued to weigh different possibilities within the contours of a united India

(Chakrabarty 2003; Roy 2009). Moreover, the idea of Pakistan found initial support not in the provinces of Bengal and Punjab where Muslims were a majority but in the UP where they were a minority. It was not until early 1947 that some Punjabi and Bengali Hindus sided with the idea of a partitioned India over that of a united India.

Pakistan meant different things to different groups of Muslims and not all of them supported the idea. For rural Bengalis, Pakistan was a 'peasant utopia' that promised freedom from Hindu landlord domination (Hashmi 1992). For minority Muslims in the UP and Bihar, it evoked the idea of a 'new Medina' (Dhulipala 2014). Its geographical contours were deliberately vague to allow those who supported the concept to project their ideas onto it. Whatever the meanings and imaginings, it was not until the mid-1940s that the idea of Pakistan became synonymous with the Partition.

History is often at odds with both the official and public memory of the Partition. In the case of the subcontinent, the narrative of nationhood determines and differentiates such memories depending on one's regional location. For Indians, remembering the Partition means recalling the dark side of Independence, a moment of loss, a moment when not only was the country divided but families separated, exiled, and forced out of homelands into 'foreign' lands. In contrast,

Pakistanis remember 1947 as the year when a religiously informed nation, homeland, and identity were realized for minority Muslims in British India. For Muslims, the Partition is framed as 'independence' from the perceived threat of Hindu majoritarianism. The reality that not all Muslims aligned themselves with such an idea or moved to Pakistan after 1947 detracts little from this memory of the Partition (Qasmi and Robb 2017). In Bangladesh, the memory of 1947 has been almost erased by the substitution with another partition, that of 1971. Rather than highlight the limits of religious nationalism, the narrative of Bangladeshi nationhood has ensured that it traces a linear history based on Muslim Bengali ethnic identity from 1905 when Lord Curzon partitioned the Bengal Presidency (Feldman 1999).

One of the consequences of such broad-ranging and often incompatible narratives has been the continuation of self-reflexive nationalisms and confrontation politics between India, Pakistan, and Bangladesh. Strained political relations have impacted the very study of the Partition by hampering dialogue and access between and among scholars from different countries. However, the tide seems to be turning as recent scholars have embarked on cross-border studies to bring us new ways to trace Partition narratives based on commonality and connection in spite of international borders (Zamindar 2007; Roy 2012).

Beyond causality, responsibility, and the politics of the Partition, scholars have, in the past two decades, focused on the human experience of the Partition. Why did people decide to move and what was the experience of migration? What did families experience being divided? What were the different experiences of refugees and migrants? How was violence experienced, perpetrated, and by whom? How do memories of 1947 frame our present post-colonial states? Seeking answers to such questions has taken scholars outside of the archives to examine and compare representations in literature and the arts (Didur 2006; Daiya 2008; Saint 2010; Sengupta 2015; Mookerjea-Leonard 2017). They have focused on the experience of women as victims—not only of physical violence but also of patriarchal understandings of their bodies within their own families, communities, and nation states. The experience of violence has generated enquiries on how intergenerational memories and forgetting of such trauma lead to specific forms of 'post-amnesias' that frame understandings of the Partition (Kabir 2013).

Representations of the human experience of the Partition soon after the Partition are immortalized in stories of writers such as Sadat Hasan Manto, Ismat Chugtai, Bapsi Sidhwa, Atin Bandyopadhya, Jyotirmayee Devi, and many others. Films such as *Garam Hawa* and *Meghey Dhaka Tara* represented the

9

plight of the refugees and the framing of national identities. Recent efforts have been directed towards collecting oral narratives of those who lived through those years. These have provided a more complete depiction of the experiences of violence, rapes, and uprooting and provide us with everyday experiences of people during the Partition (Talbot and Tatla 2006; Kaur 2007; Virdee 2013).

This shift in questions about the Partition has drawn significant attention to the disjunction between nationalized histories and the personal narratives of 1947. They highlight how collective and individual memories of Partition violence are mediated along caste, class, and gendered lines. In giving voice and agency to non-elite Indians and Pakistanis, such a shift has to grapple with some uncomfortable conclusions. For example, the human experiences of Partition violence indicate that not everyone was a victim; some individuals were perpetrators (Butalia 1998). While acknowledging other factors such as the role of grass-roots leaders, complicity of partisan members of the police and the military, and the failure of the British colonial state to protect the people, the fact remains that Partition violence pitted neighbours, friends, and communities against each other (Khan 2007).

Including all human experiences also broadens the narrative of the Partition that had been primarily concentrated on Hindus, Muslims, and Sikhs, and accounts that were limited to upper-caste and upper-class memories. Recent histories of the Partition have attempted to render those who had been invisible in the earlier narrative—the untouchables or the Dalits—more visible, to suggest differences within the Partition experience. The focus on Dalit politics in the run-up to the Partition, their experiences of migration and violence, and within the Indian state's rehabilitation efforts are significant not only in revising the erasure but also in complicating the histories of the Partition (Rawat 2001; Bandyopadhyay 2004; Sen 2014).

This book suggests that there are three different and overlapping narratives of the Partition of India, all of which need to be taken into account for a comprehensive understanding of 1947 and beyond. Revisiting the political aspects of the division have commanded the most interest and is the most common way of unravelling why and what happened during the Partition. Analysis of the long-term and short-term causes, the high politics behind closed doors, and the political articulations within a limited colonial civil sphere that dovetailed with mass politics help us to attribute responsibility for the division. Whichever way one frames these 'causes'—as the culmination of communalism based on region and religion, as the breakdown of infrastructure and consequence of the logic of the decolonization process, or as the birth pangs of newly forming nation states—the political narrative provides us crucial but still partial insight into the process of division.

This brings us to the second way of understanding the Partition. Beyond the political experience, the Partition had a significant human dimension that did not always follow the expected results of the political processes and often went contrary to it. No one, other than probably B. R. Ambedkar, had envisaged the impact that the political decision to partition would have on the people on the ground. In hindsight, this may seem foolish, given the communally charged environment in the 1940s and the contingencies that accompanied the months leading up to August 1947. As millions moved across newly created borders, uncertain about their future, violence became a way in which such uncertainties manifested in the people. Violence engulfed and affected large groups, irrespective of caste, class, religion, and gender. Specific violence targeting women was a new phenomenon in the subcontinent. The experience of becoming refugees, of citizenship, or perceived enemies in one's own homeland often defied official efforts and exhortations.

In this context, it would be useful to point out that when we think about the Partition of India we should consider two different regional experiences in Bengal and Punjab and avoid privileging one experience as normative. Thus, horrific violence, mass-scale and swift migration of communities, and near success in the rehabilitation of refugees were the key markers in Punjab. In Bengal, the trajectories were different. Here, violence was small-scale and routine, and migration, although large in numbers, was chronic yet long term. While the borders between India and West Pakistan became closed and surveilled, those in the eastern sector remained open and porous for decades. The Indian state declared its efforts at refugee rehabilitation a success for Punjabi refugees while the case for Bengali refugees was deemed a failure. Regional political identity in the post-1947 decades was indelibly shaped by such different experiences.

A third way to understand the Partition would be to understand its legacies and memories. Rather than seeing the Partition as a singular watershed moment ending British rule, heralding Independence, and giving birth to two distinct sovereignties, it would be useful to connect continuities, both temporally and between the two new nation states. The series of political processes, cultural understandings, and religious differences that led up to 1947 continued, acquiring new frameworks after 1947. The Partition also continued within the efforts of India and a divided Pakistan to build new nations and frame new states, through the movement of refugees and migrants—which often tested those very efforts—and in the memories and representations of those who experienced these processes in different ways.

People in the subcontinent and their diaspora worldwide inhabit a world that remains profoundly shaped by the events and experiences of 1947 and its aftermath. The legacies of the Partition continue to impact ongoing political conflicts, frame understandings of communal relationships between Hindus and Muslims, and create and influence memories and stories within families who remain divided across borders. One of the goals of this short introduction is to remind us that 70 years down the road, the narrative of the Partition is very much with us, being actively framed through international diplomacy and wars and through collective post-memories (Hirsch 2012) and post-amnesias (Kabir 2013).

The book directs our attention both to the promises of new nation states and their limitations. It challenges the popular understanding of the Partition as the culmination of a civilizational clash between Hinduism and Islam. Instead the book urges the reader to consider the historical context, contingency, nuance, and diversity of political imperatives that informed and shaped the events of 1947 and its aftermath. Most importantly, it insists on acknowledging the costs incurred by the partition in India, Pakistan, and Bangladesh, in terms of the millions of people who lost their lives and the millions more who were uprooted and exiled from their homelands. In introducing the distinct aspects of the Partition, the reader is urged to reflect on the multiplicity of meanings of 1947 and its relevance in framing and understanding the challenges faced in South Asia today.

1

The Road to Partition

Partition was not the inevitable result of intransigent differences between the Hindus and Muslims of British India. The road to Partition was paved with the multiple and contextual understandings of the two nations, the structural paradoxes of late nineteenth-century social and political formations, and also by the fact that such processes of community formation were complemented by dominant British understandings of India's communities (Bose and Jalal 2011).

However, one of the popular assumptions about the causes of the Partition stresses on the problematic assumption that the 'two-nation' theory, which claimed that Indian Muslims were a distinctive and separate community, was key to the division. In Pakistan, official histories link this theory with their 'origin' story. A counterargument, developed by Indian nationalist historians, seeks to blame the policy of 'divide and rule' under the British, which divided Hindus and Muslims, who had, until colonial rule, been tied by history, language, and culture.

Both arguments need contextualization within the long- and short-term trajectories permeating the social and political landscape of colonial India. British understandings of India as a region comprising Hindus and Muslims as distinct, homogeneous, and antagonistic communities were critical in shaping the policies of political representation. Census operations lent validity and created distinct understandings of 'majority' and 'minority' communities. Throughout the late nineteenth and the first half of the twentieth centuries, such policies in some senses aided and abetted the rivalry and competition among different religious groups, reinforcing the idea of Hindu and Muslim antagonisms.

Ironically, reform and revivalist trends within each community also tended to frame their communities as monolithic and homogeneous. Late nineteenth-century Muslim revivalist movements such as the Fariazi or the Deoband programmes provided, in their articulation of socio-economic discontents, some measure of regional and religious unity to the Muslim communities in India (Metcalf 1982; Jalal 2000). Similarly, late nineteenth-century Hindu revivalism under the banners of the Arya Samaj in Punjab and the neo-Vaishnavism in Bengal sought to frame Hindu consciousness as exclusive, devoid of its syncretic identity, and in opposition to a perception of 'Muslim tyranny' (Sarkar 1983). However, such coherence remained fractured along caste, class and *biradari* (fraternity, kinsfolk, extended family), regional, and linguistic lines, and partially shaped by patterns of social and economic relations linked to colonial rule. Thus, a religiously informed cultural identity was one of the many identities one had and it was impossible to predict which ones would achieve primacy in the late colonial period.

It is also worth noting from the outset that the 'two-nation theory' meant different things to different groups, and needs to be placed within other sociopolitical trends of the time. Indian Muslims, like any other group, were fragmented along class, language, ethnic, and sectarian lines. The major cultural divide was between the *ashraf* (descendants of Arab, Afghan, and Turkish invaders) and the *ailaf* (converts from indigenous populations). In Bengal, elite Muslims were divided into the urban Urdu-speaking professionals and the rural landlords, who spoke Bengali similar to the Muslim peasant labourers and artisans in the region (Ahmed 1988; Bandyopadhyay 2004). Further, they were united only by a vague allegiance to the essentials of Islam. In Punjab, migration and conversation had created an Islamic community that shared the Punjabi language and cultural traditions with the Hinduism, Sikhism, and Sufism (Gilmartin 1989). Thus, such efforts to forge community identities based on religion sometimes resulted in agrarian radicalism as in eastern Bengal or in attempts to return to pure Islam as in Punjab.

By the late colonial period, economic grievances, rapid urbanization, and the emergence of an industrial workforce created ambiguous and complex rifts between Hindus and Muslims (Freitag 1992). A sense of relative economic deprivation, lack of educational opportunities and consequent participation within the colonial body politic, and social imbalances vis-á-vis the Hindu upper and middle castes were influential in framing the short-term context for the 1930s and 1940s. More importantly, in both Bengal and Punjab, after the provincial elections of 1937, the Congress High Command's refusal to acknowledge the League's demands as politically credible would be the turning point on which the road to Independence would also veer towards Pakistan and Partition.

In this chapter, we will examine some of these arguments and outline some of the long-term and short-term trajectories that will provide a multi-layered narrative of the diverse paths that culminated in the

Partition. The *longue durée* approach suggests that the 'two-nation' idea was a pragmatic vision of a pluralistic society, an essential re-crafting to address the paradoxes of colonial modernity. The short-term focus on late colonial politics helps us examine the contingent paths of separate electorates and exclusionary mass politics of the 1930s and 1940s.

'Majorities and Minorities' in British India

The British understanding that Indian Muslims were a distinct, homogeneous political community came to be after the Mutiny of 1857. British officials perceived the Muslim landed elite as natural allies and as counterweights to both Muslim lower classes, who they saw as prone to religious revivalism and 'fanaticism', and educated Hindu middle classes (Sarkar 1983; Bose and Jalal 2011). For example, British ideas promoted in W. W. Hunter's *Indian Mussalmans* were critical in advancing the idea of a homogeneous and 'backward' Muslim community that was prone to sedition. Hunter identified the upper-class Muslims as natural leaders who should not only adopt Western knowledge but also acquaint themselves with their own religious mores to be able to command respect within the Muslim community (Hunter 1871). Viceroy Dufferin extended this idea of cultural homogeneity by referring to Muslims as a 'nation of fifty million' in 1888 (Sarkar 1983).

British census operations in 1872 and 1881 paradoxically revealed the wide social, regional, and class differences between Muslims in British India. It showed that in the UP, Muslims constituted only 13 per cent of the population and belonged mostly to the aristocratic ashraf class, who spoke Urdu. In Punjab and Bengal, on the other hand, Muslims and Hindus were numerically equal at 51 per cent and 49 per cent respectively. The Muslim majority comprised primarily of poor peasants and agricultural labourers who spoke their regional languages of Punjabi and Bengali respectively. Thus, the rural, largely impoverished Muslims in these regions had little in common with elite ashraf Muslims in the UP and Bihar. In addition, Muslims in Bengal and those in Punjab had very little in common with each other by way of practices, language, and culture.

Despite such clear sectarian, linguistic, and cultural differences, the British viewed the 19.7 per cent Muslims of British India as homogeneous, a community that was alternatively a 'nation' and a 'minority' with shared religious and social customs, and a common memory. The census lent scientific credibility not only to numerical sizes of religious communities, but also to the mistaken understanding that people of each

21

community, so articulated, shared common interests and had uniform social and religious customs (Cohn 1998).

On their part, the Muslim elite were not only keen to safeguard their interests, but were also willing to make certain accommodations with the British that would guarantee their participation in political decisions affecting the control of social resources. One of the key proponents of this alliance with the British was Sir Syed Ahmed Khan, the founder of the Aligarh Muslim University, who stressed the virtues and benefits of a Western education. Khan offered a loyalist path to the traditional elite, Muslim landlords and service gentry, who faced a decline because the Hindu merchant and service class were increasingly gaining power in their economic and administrative universe. Khan's efforts towards English education were focused on constructing an idea of Muslim solidarity and the notion of community (*qaum*) (Banerjee-Dube 2015). Additionally, he aimed to impress upon the British the need to view the significance of the Muslim community in political rather than numerical terms. Khan's views were not representative of the views of the Indian Muslims. Many competing narratives of belonging were framed along linguistic, regional, and class lines and these contested the idea of a universal and separate 'Muslim' identity.

Muslim identity did not rest solely on Islam in the second half of the nineteenth century (Hasan 1993). But there was a sense of community, however fuzzy, that was fostered in distinct ways through the efforts of reformers, religious teachers, travel, and local cultural efforts. Efforts to frame community identity came from within as some focused on a return to the fundamentals of Islam and on purifying Islam of its Western and Hindu influences. In Bengal, a small Muslim elite encouraged the institution of Islamic schools, which would standardize religious education and help preserve the distinctive linguistic and cultural identity of the Bengali Muslims (Sengupta 2011). In northern India, revivalist movements such as those associated with the Deoband School began reassessing the parameters of authentic religion through a focus on classical Islamic texts, laying emphasis on notions of charisma and highlighting certain aspects of Sufi traditions. However, they also adopted British–style classrooms and promoted Urdu as a language of prose, and enlisted membership through subscriptions and community meetings (Metcalf 1982). Thus, they claimed to speak for 'tradition' within the context of colonial modernity and remained, in contrast to Syed Ahmed Khan's loyalism, deeply anti–British.

The constructions of communal identities were not restricted to Muslims in this period. Hindus adopted similar religious self-strengthening efforts by incorporating devotional theism and encouraging a return to the fundamental ideas within Hinduism. In Punjab and the North Western Frontier Provinces (NWFP), the Arya Samaj of Dayanand Saraswati viewed India as essentially Hindu. It redefined Hinduism through its opposition to caste, idols, and temples, and sought to create an open social system where individuals would be defined by education and achievements rather than by their inherited caste identity. The Arya Samaj's concern about creating a robust, healthy nation to counter a masculine West as well as the threat of numerical depletion was reflected in their efforts to purify (*shuddhi*) and reclaim those who had previously converted to Islam, Christianity, or Sikhism (Malhotra 2004).

In Punjab, the activities of the Singh Sabha Movement contributed to the framing of a unified identity among Sikhs. The movement discouraged heterogeneity by going back to the fundamental teachings of the Sikh gurus and tried to establish strict norms and codes of conduct within the community. Attempts to establish a normative Sikh tradition were focused on creating distinctions between hitherto syncretic traditions between Hindus and Sikhs. Reformers discouraged Sikhs from participating in Hindu festivals such as Holi and from making pilgrimages to non-Sikh shrines (Oberoi 1997).

In Bengal, devotional messages of reformed Guadiya Vaishnavism found renewed approval among educated, middle-class Bengalis, hoping not only to recover traditions, but also to engage with colonial modernity. Gaudiya Vaishnavism was, therefore, recast as specifically modern—a devotional, monotheistic, Sanskritic religious tradition—and as an integral and formative constituent of Bengali Hindu culture (Bhatia 2017). The teachings of Vivekananda presented Vedantic Hinduism as a universal faith and emphasized a 'muscular spirituality' that reflected India's cultural superiority over the West (Banerjee 2005).

While religion and caste offered crucial elements for the construction of community identity, economic realities were key to such processes. For example, the onset of colonialism caused severe economic and social dislocation of groups such as weavers and spinners, primarily Muslim, in northern India. They had little protection from market forces dominated by adverse trade policies and machine-made products. Consequently, such Muslims became increasingly indebted to moneylenders, bankers, and big merchants, who were usually Hindu. Similarly, Hindu peasants had to deal with revenue demands from Hindu *talukdar*s and landlords (Sarkar 1983). Efforts to create community identity on the basis of religion thus often found easy reception and alignment with class grievances.

It was not until the 1880s that such socio-economic differences combined with the efforts to forge religiously distinct communities coincided and manifested themselves through conflict. Scholars have conclusively shown that 'communal' riots, particularly in Punjab, eastern UP, and Bihar, increased exponentially from the 1880s and were often centred on issues perceived as religious grievances, such as cow protection (Sarkar 1983; Pandey 1992; Adcock 2010). Between 1880 and 1895, the largest number of riots focused on the issue of cow slaughter despite the rapid rise of Hindu cow-protection societies in northern and western India. Further, communal tensions were heightened by Bal Gangadhar Tilak's reorganization of the Ganapati festival as a community celebration that urged Hindus to boycott Muslim festivals such as Muharram in which they had freely participated before. In the last decade of the nineteenth century, the suburbs of Calcutta saw large-scale riots over such issues as Bakr Id and cow protection between different sections of the industrial working class.

Such communal riots highlight the close yet contradictory relationship of the framing of community identity along religious and class lines that allowed mill workers, peasants, and artisans to see themselves as part of the wider religious community that contained their elite compatriots. Although reform and revival efforts in the second half of the nineteenth century among Hindus and Muslims failed to crystallize their identity into unified and homogeneous blocks, colonial understandings of Indian society viewed such disputes around cow protection and socio-economic inequalities as examples of continuing strife between two historically antagonistic communities.

Separate Electorates and the Politics of Representation

The colonial state's introduction of representative institutions, their controversial decision to partition their largest province in Bengal in 1905, and the founding of the League in Dacca (Dhaka) in 1906 combined and strengthened the idea that Hindus and Muslims had different identities and distinct political priorities. In the first two decades of the twentieth century, the emerging anti-colonialism of both Hindus and Muslims was influenced by their religious ideas and symbols. Given that the census operations had declared the Hindus to be a 'majority' community, Hindu majoritarian impulses and iconographies easily dominated the framing of such anti-colonial discourse. Consequently, Muslims, enumerated as a 'minority' community by the colonial state, found it increasingly difficult to be accepted as both Muslims and as anti-colonial nationalists, even as they tried to make common cause with the Congress. Thus, in 1912, Mohammed Ali argued that the educated Hindu 'communal patriot' had effectively managed to use Hinduism and its symbols for mobilizing the masses and imagining the Indian nation but 'refused to give quarter to the Muslims unless the latter quietly shuffles off his individuality and becomes completely Hinduized' (Ali 1988). However, these decades also saw potentials and actualities of Hindu–Muslim political unity as representatives joined together to pressure the Raj to expand the electorate and to demand self-government.

From the late nineteenth century, Muslim leadership had demanded separate reservations for Muslims within the colonial infrastructure to redress the growing lags in education and employment and to protect them from Hindu competition. They also demanded separate electorates to ensure that Muslim representatives in electoral bodies would be proportionate and be elected by Muslim voters alone. For the British, anxious to make peace between perceived homogeneous communities and to have a counterweight to the growing critique of colonial rule, adopting the principle of maintaining a balance between Hindus and Muslims was a great solution. Consequently, in 1885, the British passed a resolution to ensure that Muslims had proper representation in government services. In 1897, a government circular followed the resolution directing the government of the largest province in British India, Bengal, to fill up two-thirds of its vacancies in the lower rungs of administration through direct nominations of Muslims so that a balance in representation could be achieved between Hindus and Muslims (Banerjee-Dube 2015).

This set the context for the Partition of Bengal in 1905, which created a new province of Eastern Bengal and Assam, which had a Muslim majority to ensure a greater share of power for the community there. Although the British justified the division on grounds of administrative efficiency, it was clearly a political move to divide the growing opposition to British rule. Viceroy Lord Curzon urged the Muslim landed elites in Bengal to see the benefits of the division. While this fuelled the development of Muslim separatism, there is also evidence that both Hindus and Muslims came together under the banner of common language to agitate against the Partition of 1905. Beyond Bengal, students at Aligarh passed a resolution in 1906 advocating Hindu–Muslim political cooperation for the swadeshi cause. Further, initial phases of the resistance enjoyed Muslim participation even as such resistance went against the economic interests of Bengal's rural poor, a majority of whom were Muslims.

However, such Hindu–Muslim accord was a cause for concern for both the Muslim elites in Bengal and the UP and the British. The former sent a deputation to Viceroy Minto, Curzon's successor, urging for separate political recognition based on community identity and that 'minority groups' have proportional representation in public employment and within representative government. The viceroy assured the deputation that he would safeguard the rights of East Bengali Muslims. In December 1906, a group of elite Muslims, invigorated with their recent successes with the colonial government, established a separate political party—the All India Muslim League—in Dacca. The key agenda was to safeguard the interests and political rights of Muslims in India and to preach loyalty to British rule.

The India Councils Act of 1909, also known as the Morley–Minto Reforms, provided limited self-government to Indians by increasing the electorate of the lower legislative councils. More significantly, it testified to the League's success in gaining official recognition as a significant political minority. The reforms granted separate electorates to Muslims and granted them extra seats commensurate with their political significance in provinces in which they were a minority. The principle of separate electorates prevented possible combinations of Indians in the lower councils that could oppose the British, who retained the majority of seats in the Imperial Legislative Council.

Muslim representation in the imperial and legislative councils exceeded their actual numbers in the general population, reflecting the British understanding of their political significance. Moreover, elections were constrained severely by income: Muslims with a certain income were entitled to vote while Hindus with the same income were estimated too poor to qualify (Banerjee-Dube 2015).

The next stage of constitutional reforms, the Montagu–Chelmsford Reforms of 1919, continued to support the case for separate electorates even as it continued to expand the electorate. The 1920s and early 1930s, however, were a low point for the League. The Montagu–Chelmsford Reforms had shifted the balance of the franchise towards the landed, so the Muslim platform had to give way to landed parties. It would not be until the Government of India Act of 1935, which granted provincial autonomy, that the League would find it possible to actually translate some of its demands into political reality.

Several other trends during World War I and the 1920s belie the trajectory of an inevitable road to

Partition. The annulment of the Partition of Bengal in 1911 not only showed the inconsistent nature of British rule, but also allowed space for collaboration between moderates in the Congress, such as G. K. Gokhale and Bal Gangadhar Tilak, and members of the League, such as Mohammed Ali Jinnah and Saifuddin Kichlu. Together, they hoped to bring pressure on the British to expand electorates in all councils, to grant general franchise, and to introduce a separate electorate for Muslims, with provision for representation corresponding to weightage in minority provinces. In this respect, the League adopted self-government as one of its primary political goals from 1913 and its leaders called for Hindu–Muslim political unity.

Efforts at political unity coexisted with new trends in pan-Islamism. Britain's alienation from Turkey and simultaneous friendship with Turkey's enemy, Russia, became a cause for concern for Indian Muslims. The Urdu press gave widespread publicity to events such as the emergence of a national movement in Egypt, Britain's refusal to interfere between Italy and Turkey, and the Young Turk Revolution in Turkey, which framed and fanned the debates on pan-Islamism and the need for Hindu–Muslim unity in colonial India. At the end of the war, such calls for cooperation bore fruit with Gandhi's support for both radical and moderate groups within the Khilafat Movement and Muslim support for the Non–Cooperation Movement between 1919 and 1922.

However, such cooperation was short-lived as Muslim liberals such as Jinnah became alienated by the growing role of religion in politics, and as the Khilafatists and the Gandhians could not come to an agreement over non-violence as a strategy. Moreover, the Congress's failure to comprehend religious community, framed within ideas of collective and political community, and the corresponding inability on the part of minority Muslims to view the Congress as their representative, hampered such efforts at unity. British recognition of religious communities as political units exacerbated the differences between the communities. Thus, in spite of imagining the nation in multiple ways, anti-colonial nationalism could never break out of the terms imposed by colonial rule. From 1922, there was a widening rift between the two communities, and, except for the NWFP and Delhi, different Muslim groups stayed away from the Congress-led anti-colonialist movements.

Provincial Elections, War, Famine, and the Pakistan Demand

It is critical to note at the outset that the idea of a religion-based territorial division was neither new in the decade before the Partition nor was it one particularly forwarded by Muslims. Fears about religious annihilation abounded among Punjabi urban Hindus who wanted to safeguard their privileges vis-á-vis those Muslims who were gaining ground in the 1920s and 1930s through British policies of communal quotas in education and representational politics. Hindu leaders such as Lajpat Rai and Swami Shradhananda had espoused the possibility of a partitioned Punjab where the eastern half would have a non-Muslim, Hindu–Sikh coalition and the western half would be governed by a Muslim government (Nair 2011). In Bengal, the middle-class, urban Hindu bhadralok similarly viewed their political future to be in jeopardy after the Communal Award of 1932 gave more seats to Muslims than Hindus in provincial legislature (Chatterji 1994). Arguably, such ideas drew their inspiration from the 1905 partition of Bengal. However, such imaginings retain the partitioned provinces within the contours of the putative Indian nation, and many Hindu, Sikh, and Muslim leaders continued to recognize the need to organize cross-communal support bases.

The same can be said about the origins of the concept of Pakistan. Meaning 'the land of the pure', Pakistan included Punjab, the NWFP, Kashmir, Sindh, and Baluchistan, and had its origins in 1933. It did not find popular acceptance and the elite Muslim leaders largely regarded it as impractical. As a conceptual homeland for Muslims, it did not advocate for a division but was to be a unifying idea for Indian Muslims. It was not until after World War II that the demand for a separate Muslim homeland was linked to the possibility of partition. Wartime pressures and the promise that the British would quit India created contingent contexts that made such linkages possible. To understand how it came to be in the short term, one needs to begin with the Government of India Act of 1935.

The Government of India Act of 1935, in some ways, set the stage for the growing schism between Hindus and Muslims in the late 1930s. The Act, which introduced representative government at the provincial level, projected a future federation in which representatives of the princely states would be a counterbalance to the elected representatives in British India. The Act, a classic example of political engineering by the colonial state, gave concessions at the provincial level without giving up control at the centre while reserving vital attributes of sovereignty and control over India's finances and defence for the British. Moreover, the rules of representation were deliberately laid down to negate the possibility of a nationalist majority in the projected federal legislature, prompting Jawaharlal Nehru to denounce the Act as a 'new charter of slavery' (Nehru 1975).

More importantly, the Act granted separate electorates to the Muslims and reserved seats for the Scheduled Castes in the provincial and central legislatures. It directed the political attention of all major political groups in India towards the provinces by announcing that elections would take place in 1937. An increased number of propertied Indians, around 35 million (about 10 per cent of the total), would be able to vote in these upcoming elections.

The 1937 elections resulted in a Congress victory in 8 out of the 11 provinces and it won 711 out of the 1,585 contested seats. It won absolute majorities in Madras, Bihar, Orissa, Central Provinces, and the UP, a near majority in Bombay, and emerged as the largest party in Assam, Bengal, and the NWFP. But it fared badly in Punjab and Sind. On its part, the League won only 108 of the 485 possible Muslims seats and performed badly in Muslim-majority provinces such as Sind, Punjab, the NWFP, and Bengal. The fact that the League did not win a single seat in the NWFP and got only two in Punjab and three in Sind suggests that it barely had any presence in the Muslim-majority provinces. The election results negated the League's claim of being the sole party to represent Muslim interests.

The true winners of the provincial elections were the regional parties in the Muslim-majority provinces of Bengal and Punjab—the Krishak Praja Party (KPP) and the Unionist Party respectively. The Unionist Party, led by Fazl-i-Husain, Sikander Hayat Khan, and Jat leader Chotu Ram, represented the interests of the Muslims, the Sikh landed gentry, and peasant producers (Talbot 1988). In Bengal, Fazlul Haq's KPP successfully appealed to Muslims and lower-caste Hindu peasants to put their class-based concerns over the needs of communal unity.

The 1937 elections revealed several significant patterns that would frame the political campaigns and participation in the coming decade. It became clear that the League received most of its support in Muslim-minority provinces, where it projected itself as the guardian of the community. In the Muslim-majority provinces, such as in Bengal and Punjab, the pattern of voting demonstrated that the Muslim electorate was moved more by local and regional issues than by national ones. In these provinces, community identity continued to intersect in different ways with economic and linguistic identities. What the elections also revealed was the Congress's limited appeal to Muslim voters in spite of its Muslim mass contact movement earlier in 1937 (Hasan 1993).

In spite of its limited appeal among Muslim groups, the Congress continued to claim to represent all communities, and offered to share the government in the UP with the League leaders if they ceased to function as a separate group. Such insistence on total absorption, while strategically sound, created alienation among Muslims in the province. Less justifiably, in Bengal and Punjab, the Congress rebuffed the efforts to form governments with the regional parties, Fazlul Haq's KPP and the Unionist Party respectively, forcing these parties to seek alliances with the League.

The rejection of a political coalition in these key provinces was a great blunder and clearly widened the ideological and political distance between Hindus and Muslims. In fact, the secularist and radical rhetoric of the Congress during the mass contact campaigns alarmed Muslim vested interests without winning over the Muslim masses. The increasing prominence of the Hindu Mahasabha, the emergence of the Rashtriya Swayam Sevak Sangh (RSS), and their adoption of uncompromising Hindu communalism created the spectre of Hindu domination within the Muslim electorate. This was further accentuated in the UP as the new administration enforced cow protection and the use of Hindi. Concurrently, the election results of 1937 galvanized the League leaders to build up a more populist image. The League accepted complete independence with effective minority safeguards as its creed and denounced the Congress for creating 'class bitterness and communal war' (Sarkar 1983). In 1938,

Jinnah demanded that the League be recognized as the sole representative of the Muslims—a claim that would remain unjustified until the mid-1940s.

At the Lahore session of the League in 1940, Jinnah's presidential speech spelled out the two-nation theory justification for a separate Muslim homeland. He stated that Muslims and Hindus were separate culturally, in their historical memory, and were opposed, monolithic religious communities. Thus, in Jinnah's argument, no settlement between the two could be reached that would satisfy the aspirations of the Muslims. Although neither Pakistan nor partition is mentioned by name, the resolution has subsequently been dubbed as the 'Pakistan resolution' and often mistakenly seen as the blueprint for Pakistan. Few Muslim leaders took Pakistan literally and even for Jinnah it was more of a bargaining chip in his negotiations with the British and the Congress (Jalal 1985). The Lahore Resolution framed the Muslims as a 'nation' and not a 'minority'. It urged for a Muslim homeland to be constituted in the Muslim-majority provinces in north-west and north-east India. The sovereignty and the constitution of these states and their relation to India were to be decided in the future.

Two things are important at this point: dissolution of the unitary centre and its reconstitution based on agreements that included the Muslim-majority provinces and the princely states; and the recognition of the political validity of a separate state comprising principal Muslim provinces. Jinnah's demand also aimed for a new framing of the constitutional arrangements in which Muslims would have equal share—a partnership between two nations, Pakistan and Hindustan. For Jinnah, recourse to religion to define political community was a pragmatic measure and he deliberately kept the idea of 'Pakistan' vague to garner the maximum Muslim support (Jalal 1985).

India's automatic involvement in World War II in 1939—without any consultation—saw different mobilizations on the part of the Congress and the League. Initially, the Congress demanded that in exchange for supporting British war efforts, the British would have to agree to an immediate national government at the centre and promise independence after the war. The British refusal led the Congress provincial ministries to resign en masse as a show of protest. The World War II years saw the Congress continue their demand for constitutional reform, mobilize their supporters to oppose colonial rule through non-cooperation and civil disobedience, and from 1942 demand that the British quit India.

In contrast, Jinnah and the League, with support from B. R. Ambedkar, hailed the resignation of the Congress ministries as a 'Day of Deliverance' (Sarkar

1983). The League offered its cooperation to the British war effort only if the rights of Muslims in India were guaranteed. Jinnah insisted on the League's status as the sole spokesperson for Indian Muslims and demanded that the League be given the right to veto future constitutional changes. Wartime expediency saw the League, along with the princes and the Unionists in Punjab, mobilized as valuable allies, who would both work for the war effort and provide an essential political buffer against the Congress's demands for new constitutional reforms.

As India's support for World War II became imperative with the threat of a Japanese invasion on the Eastern front, the British announced their intention to consider ways in which Indian demands for self-government and independence might become reality. In this context, they sent Sir Stafford Cripps, a member of the War Cabinet, to India in March 1942. Cripps's Mission is often seen as the watershed in the road to Partition. Cripps brought with him the proposal that provided for dominion status for India immediately at the end of World War II, and left India to decide whether it wished to remain within or secede from the British Commonwealth. His proposal also included a proviso that no part of India would be forced to join the post-war arrangements. More importantly, Britain would retain the responsibility for defence during

41

the World War II years, meaning that Indians would have to wait until the end of World War II to have any significant share in power.

The British plan had little room for negotiation and was rejected by almost all political parties. The Congress was dissatisfied because the plan allowed the provinces the right to be part of or remain outside the Indian Union. For the Congress, this was a great blow to the idea of Indian unity. Gandhi saw the mission's offer as 'an invitation to the Moslems to create a Pakistan' (Talbot 2016). For the League, while the idea of non-accession was welcome, the process of exercising self-determination was limited and problematic. Ambedkar and Dalit groups did not favour it as well, viewing its safeguards to protect their rights as inadequate.

The World War II years saw the rapid rise of the League to political power, especially in provinces such as Bengal, Sind, and Assam where they were in charge by 1943. In Bengal, the KPP broke its coalition with the League by 1942, but the latter retained power under Khwaja Najimuddin thanks to the support of European MLAs and Calcutta-based elite Muslim families such as the Ispahanis. In Punjab, the League was able to gain ground against the Unionist coalition owing to weak leadership. British patronage supported the League's stature and political power, enabling it and Jinnah to demand that the party be on equal terms with the Congress. Most significantly, the League was able to popularize the demand for Pakistan, the idea of which was left deliberately ambiguous and politically abstract.

The Bengal famine of 1942, along with wartime exigencies, greatly influenced the reception of the Pakistan slogan during and after the World War II years. The Bengal famine that resulted in the death of nearly 3.5 to 3.8 million people was a man-made rather than a natural one. It was caused owing to a combination of factors such as the (un)availability of food resources, drastic declines in exchange entitlements of vulnerable social groups, and a deliberate absence of relief measures (Sen 1981). In Bengal, KPP mobilization of peasants under the rubric of economic inequalities dovetailed neatly with the numerical realities of a large Muslim peasantry dominated by Hindu landlords and moneylenders. The experience of the famine was crucial in pushing forth the communalization of class politics that framed the idea of Pakistan as a 'peasant utopia' (Hashmi 1992).

In Bengal, one needs to consider the growing integration of Scheduled Caste political representation within mainstream Hindu politics. The history of Dalit politics here had been one of protracted alienation from anti-colonial nationalism until the late 1930s. However, from this point on, scholars argue, 'religion' replaced 'caste' as the defining criterion for Schedule Caste political community and they became integrated within mainstream Hindu politics (Bandyopadhyay 1997, 2004; Chatterjee 1998). Consequently, Dalits in Bengal not only supported the Congress and the Hindu Mahasabha's campaigns to partition the province but were also both perpetrators and victims of subsequent communal violence.

However, at the all-India level, Dalit integration into national politics was not complete or straightforward. Thus, in the UP, the Dalits demanded a parallel 'Achutistan' or a homeland, separate from the Congress's and the League's demands (Rawat 2001). In other parts of northern India and Punjab, Ambedkar and the Scheduled Castes Federation became a popular alternative to pre-existing regional movements around Dalit identity. However, these became subsumed within mainstream Congress politics owing to factionalism and lack of organization and resources (Lynch 1969; Juergensmeyer 1982). More significantly, although the Dalits were a sizeable minority at the all-India level, they did not constitute a significant majority in any single province. This meant that any articulation of national community found it difficult to link territory with it (Rao 2009).

Thus, representative politics in late colonial India remained divided along religious, caste, and regional lines. In Bengal, the rising political popularity of the Hindu Mahasabha during the World War II years, and in Punjab, the Sikh opposition to the League's Pakistan demands and their willingness to ally with the Congress greatly hampered any potential for political accommodations between different religious communities. The same is true for regional League branches in these two provinces, which often put regional interests over national ones. However, at the national level, by 1945, Jinnah was successful in shifting the conversation about Indian Muslims as a 'minority' to one that framed them as a 'nation'. Congress politics remained focused on demanding representative power at every level and there was little indication that Partition was around the corner. At the popular level, the spectacular popularity of the idea of Pakistan among Muslims ran counter to the increasingly strident efforts of the Hindu Mahasabha, particularly in Bengal and Punjab, leading to antagonism between the communities.

The Road to Catastrophe

Ironically, it was the veteran Congress leader C. Rajagopalachari's plan in 1944 that clearly articulated the possibility of a partition and of Pakistan through a division of provinces. According to this plan, the

Congress would agree to the demand for Pakistan by carving out the Muslim-majority parts from the provinces of Bengal and Punjab. This 'Pakistan' would have to seek common arrangements such as defence, communications, and commerce with the rest of India. But such a partition did not promise equal political parity for Muslims. Jinnah dismissed the plan as offering the Muslims a 'maimed, mutilated and moth eaten Pakistan' (Jalal 1985). Further, it is worthwhile to consider that at this point, Jinnah's demands for parity between Hindus and Muslims envisaged Muslims belonging collectively within India without being situated in separate sovereign nation states (Banerjee-Dube 2015).

The demand for Pakistan, as a political entity with equal parity within India or as a separate nation, dominated the fast-moving political negotiations between 1946 and the early months of 1947. In hindsight, it is clear that for Jinnah, plans would necessarily require the partitioning of Bengal and Punjab. At the time, such prospects created tensions among the non-Muslims in Bengal and Punjab, which their respective governors warned about in their communications to authorities in London and Delhi. Furthermore, the British refused to dispel the popular perception among the Muslims that Pakistan would include most, if not all, of Punjab and Bengal. For its part, the Congress continued to reiterate their policy that any solution to the Hindu–Muslim problem would have to wait until Independence.

The 1946 provincial elections changed the status quo substantially as Jinnah and the League won all the Muslim seats to the central assembly and received 75 per cent of the total Muslim vote in the provincial assembly elections. The reasons for the win lie in the rapidly changing local and regional contexts during and after the World War II, and in the ability of the provincial League leaders to form coalitions with local leaders. The League's win in Punjab, described as the 'cornerstone of Pakistan' by Jinnah, was a direct result of Jinnah's ability to take advantage of factional rivalries (Talbot 1990). Furthermore, the League's efforts to appeal directly to the religious sentiments of the Muslim peasants, incorporating the support of the rural aristocracy and religious leaders, paid huge dividends during the election. The grand coalition of the Unionist Party suffered a defeat as landlords and *pir*s (spiritual guide and elder) decided to withdraw their support.

In Bengal, the faction of the League led by Abul Hashim managed to reap rewards for its role in famine relief at a time when many Muslims peasants were victims of black-market racketeering by Hindu traders and landlords. The mass mobilization campaigns, which spread the idea of Pakistan as a moral, economic, and political panacea, resulted in an almost universal acceptance among Bengali Muslim peasantry. The League was able to shift support from the KPP to itself and gain an overwhelming victory.

On its part, the Congress emerged as the most significant representative of India as it swept the 'general' constituencies and got 91.3 per cent of the non-Muslim votes. The election results also show a complete routing of the Hindu Mahasabha, the Scheduled Castes Federation, and the Communists, indicating the hegemonic hold of the Congress.

At this juncture, in March 1946, the Cabinet Mission arrived in India to negotiate the terms of transfer of power. It was headed by Sir Pethick-Lawrence, the secretary of state for India (and Burma), and included Sir Stafford Cripps and A. V. Alexander, both high-ranking British officials. The mission had two goals—to discuss the details of framing a new constitution as a precursor to grant Indian independence and to form an interim government that would be acceptable to most of the political parties to facilitate the transfer of power. Such agreement would prove to be difficult as the Congress insisted that complete independence meant a 'united India' while the League's leaders argued that it was necessary to constitute a sovereign independent state for Muslims in order to save them from Hindu domination. This sovereign Pakistan, according to them, would be comprised of Bengal, Assam, Punjab, the NWFP, Sind, and Baluchistan.

The Cabinet Mission rejected the idea of a sovereign Pakistan and, instead, offered a loose, three-tiered federal structure for the Union of India that would include provinces as well as princely states. In this scheme, the provinces would be grouped as A (Hindu majority), B, and C (Muslim-majority provinces in the north-west and north-east including Assam), and each group could have its own executive and legislature, and the freedom to decide on what provincial subjects to handle. A Union government at the top would control defence, foreign affairs, and communication, and would be able to raise revenue. The plan envisaged the formation of an elected constituent assembly created by the newly formed provincial assemblies that would draft the constitution for the whole of India. This constitution would be reviewed in 10 years. Princely states were ensured sufficient representation in the central constituent assembly. No group or province could opt out of the proposed Indian Union. An interim government would carry on the work of everyday administration as the plan was being implemented and the wrinkles ironed out.

The Cabinet Mission plan offered Jinnah a Pakistan that did not throw away the advantages of an undivided

Punjab and Bengal. Rather, a Muslim federation would bring the Muslim provinces under the control of the League at the centre. Thus, it is not surprising that Jinnah initially accepted the plan with the caveat that Groups B and C have political parity with Group A, and that after 10 years, they have the right to secede from the Indian Union.

In contrast, the Congress found the plan problematic on three major counts. First, it did not like the condition of drafting a constitution attached to its immediate priority of getting independence. Second, it was not happy to group Assam and the NWFP, where it had majorities, with Muslim-majority provinces in Groups B and C. Third, the weak centre of the federation went against the Congress's plans that envisioned a strong centre that would guide independent India's economic development. Nehru and the Congress only offered conditional support and agreed only to participate in the constituent assembly to draft the Constitution.

The Cabinet Mission plan to form an interim government floundered on the issue of parity—the Congress insisted on including Muslim and Dalit candidates among its nominees while Jinnah wanted 5 Congress, 5 League, 1 Sikh, and 1 scheduled caste as part of the interim government. Unable to break the impasse between the Congress and the League, Viceroy Wavell set up a caretaker government consisting of

British officials in July 1946. For Jinnah, this was the last straw in a long series of obstacles set up by the Congress. The League decided to withdraw its acceptance of the Cabinet Mission plan and announced the League would use 'Direct Action' to achieve Pakistan.

The political stalemates and the failure to find a constitutional solution to transfer power once the British left brought volatility not only within high politics but also in the people's interpretation of their future. The growing realization that the British would soon leave India made many Punjabi Muslims feel that the non-communal approach to politics was no longer useful. Such assumptions were mirrored by Punjabi Hindus and Sikhs, who, fearing inclusion within the proposed Pakistan, began to argue for inclusion within India even if it meant a partition of the Punjabi homeland (Talbot 1990).

The Endgame

By early 1947, the main priority of the British was to get out of India as quickly as possible before anti-colonial politics radicalized and communal violence became uncontrollable. Prime Minister Clement Attlee announced that the British would leave India by 30 June 1948 and sent in Lord Mountbatten as the last viceroy to oversee the political disengagement.

Thus, in late March, Lord Mountbatten arrived in India with one goal in mind: Britain's quick withdrawal. After a series of talks with major political leaders and a litany of failed proposals, he proposed a plan on 3 June. Mountbatten's plan brought forward the date of independence from the earlier date of July 1948 to 15 August 1947. It declared that the Muslim-majority provinces of Bengal, Punjab, Sind, the NWFP, and Baluchistan would have the option of joining the existing constituent assembly or opting for a new one for Pakistan. The provincial assemblies would get to decide on this mandate. The Hindu-majority provinces would remain within the Indian Union. Jinnah, Nehru, and Sardar Baldev Singh on behalf of the Sikhs immediately endorsed the 3 June plan (hereinafter the Plan).

The Plan determined that British India would be partitioned into an Indian Union and a Pakistan, a homeland for Muslims. It was the work of a small group of British and Indian politicians and reflected none of the regional and local political concerns. It was based on territorial maps and census reports, a top-down conceptualization imposed by London and Delhi. Ironically, the Plan was not concerned with its potential impact on the populations that would be divided and did not have any safeguards to assuage growing public apprehensions.

The prospect of an immediate transfer of power shifted the focus from constitutional negotiations to the fate of Bengal and Punjab. Local understandings of 'freedom' and 'partition' often intersected with existing apprehensions and hopes about 'Pakistan'. In Bengal, public discourse provided and supported multiple claims: partition Bengal so that Hindus remain in India, keep Bengal united as proposed in the Plan and join Pakistan, or to create a sovereign 'United Bengal' (Roy 2009). The last, proposed by veteran Congress leader Sarat Bose and League leaders Abul Hashim and H. S. Suhrawardy, found little support from Bengali Hindus, who feared inclusion in Pakistan. Similarly, in Punjab ideas of a separate homeland for the Sikhs, the demand for Khalistan, resurfaced, along with proposals for a sovereign Punjab and a divided Punjab to ensure that minority Hindus remained in India (Nair 2011). The NWFP, not keen to join Pakistan, demanded an independent Pathan state, which was met with a forced plebiscite. The Congress ministry boycotted the plebiscite and the consequent vote of a very limited electorate sealed the fate of this region with Pakistan. Such anxieties were accentuated by the fact that neither Jinnah nor the League had ever discussed the fate of minorities within the contours of a future Pakistan (Jalal 2000).

Mountbatten's plan also included the fate of the princely states, whose rulers historically had direct treaty relations with the British crown and had traditionally been seen as allies of British rule. The Plan directed that princely states would have the option to accede either to the dominion of India or Pakistan. After 3 June, the Congress, the League, and the British directed their efforts to ensure that the princes fell in line. While princes in Bhopal, Hyderabad, and Travancore explored the possibility of retaining their autonomy, powerful people's movements in almost all princely states urged for political rights and elective representatives in the constituent assembly. Nehru classified princes who were not willing to accede to the Indian Union as 'hostile'. Mountbatten, Nehru, and the two Congress leaders, Sardar Patel and V. P Menon, charged with organizing the transfer of power for the princely states, used various methods of persuasion and coercion to bring the princely states within the fold of the Indian Union. Those who persisted in exploring alternatives, such as Hyderabad and Junagadh, faced the might of the Indian army in the immediate aftermath of Independence. In the case of Jammu and Kashmir, its accession was framed against the backdrop of armed conflict between India and Pakistan.

The accession of princely states, numbering over 550, added about half a million square miles and 90 million people to the Indian Union. As a reward for accession and giving up their autonomy, the princes were given tax-free pensions commensurate with the former state's revenue levels and some of the princes were made governors of the new administrative entities. In some ways, this integration was the most successful one within the processes that comprised the transfer of power for the Indian Union. For Pakistan, the integration of the princely states would prove to be a decade-long problem and would test its experiments with post-colonial democracy.

By June 1947, Pakistan had become a settled fact. The Bengal Assembly on 20 June and the Punjab Assembly on 23 June voted in favour of the Partition. West Punjab and East Bengal were to become part of Pakistan while East Punjab and West Bengal would remain in India. Significantly, this momentous decision came against a backdrop of large-scale communal violence in Bengal and Punjab and vocal demands for partition from Bengali and Punjabi Hindus and Sikhs, who urged their representatives to ensure that they remained within the new Indian Union. Such demands were parallel to efforts for other alternatives, but the results underline how little actual decision-making power the people of the partitioned provinces had in deciding their fates.

The Indian Independence Act was ratified by the British Crown on 18 July and implemented on 14/15 August 1947. As we shall see in the next chapter, expediency rather than accuracy guided British efforts to transfer power in 1947. Hard-fought and hard-won, India's independence did not arrive alone. 15 August and its tryst with destiny also brought with it a 'mottled dawn'.

2

A Mottled Dawn

Jawaharlal Nehru was sworn in as the prime minister of a new India in New Delhi on 15 August. Mohammed Ali Jinnah became the first president of Pakistan in a simple ceremony at Karachi the day before. While for millions these ceremonies marked the beginning of their freedom from colonial rule, for many others, large-scale uprooting, violence, and victimhood accompanied such freedom. Gandhi, totally opposed to the Partition, did not participate in the celebration and spent the day fasting and in prayer. Hindu militants affiliated with the Hindu Mahasabha and the RSS were incensed by a freedom that was accompanied by a division and campaigned against celebrations. In contrast, for Muslim ideologues who had long supported the idea of a Muslim homeland, the Partition signalled their freedom from Hindu domination.

For millions of Hindus, Muslims, and Sikhs, especially in the provinces of Bengal and Punjab, the birth of two nations created uncertainties and began a search for security and belonging in a homeland that had now been declared foreign. Not knowing whether their particular village or locality would be part of India or Pakistan, residents in Punjab and Bengal flew flags of one country or another in anticipation of being included in them only to discover later that they belonged to the other nation (Chatterji 2007; Roy 2012). The run-up to 15 August became almost nightmarish for people caught on what was potentially going to be the 'wrong' side. Lack of trust and fear within—and in between— communities was manifested in unusual and desperate measures. Some residents in Lahore and Amritsar grew or cut off their beards and learnt verses from the Kalma or the Vedas so that they could 'pass' as members of the majority community of the area. Parents sent off their unmarried daughters to cities that would clearly remain in India or Pakistan (Khan 2007).

Unsure of their changed status as minorities in India or Pakistan, people in these provinces hoped for clarification from their regional and national representatives. However, such declarations and pronouncements were not forthcoming, and when they did, it was almost always too late and inadequate. This chapter discusses the logistical processes of how the Partition came to be and how people on the ground specifically experienced it. It focuses on two critical experiences of the Partition—border making and the eruption of mass violence in Bengal and Punjab—and suggests that such experiences are not only key to understanding how the Partition played out but are also significant in explaining how national and community identities came to be re-fashioned in post-colonial India.

An Impossible Task

Once the 3 June Plan was announced and accepted, the task at hand was to divide up British India and facilitate the evacuation of the British. This meant a division of the army, governmental staff, properties, civil department records, and financial settlements, as well as a separation of the jurisdictions of high courts and federal courts, charting out domicile policies, and the delineation of the new borders. In the true spirit of British efficiency, a Partition Committee, later replaced by a Partition Council on 26 June 1947, was created to divide the assets and liabilities. It was steered by two civil servants—a Hindu, H. M. Patel, and a Muslim, Chaudhuri Mohammad Ali. Ten expert committees, whose membership included an equal number of high-ranking Hindu and Muslim bureaucrats representing the interests of the future India and Pakistan, assisted the Council. An arbitral tribunal was convened in anticipation of disputes between both sides. Similar council structures were put into place at the provincial level. A general rule of thumb was to guide the division; physical and moveable goods would be divided along statistical lines, with 80 per cent going to India and 20 per cent to Pakistan. Every item of government property was itemized and listed to facilitate the division. On the face of it, the task of partition was to be an organized and orderly affair until the last official paper clip was divided equitably (Sengupta 2014).

The reality was far from such expectations. The committees had around eight weeks to conclude their task. The mandate to divide up government assets required fully functioning capital cities in Karachi and Dacca. However, creating infrastructure for the full functioning of a government was a daunting task. New buildings had to be built while old buildings were requisitioned and repaired to make them suitable as seats of political power. Everything, from accommodation and salaries to simple government stationery, had to be created anew. The irony of the task is clear when one focuses on the Council's mandate to divide up historical monuments and objects. The terms of the division were such that India would become the repository of a rich Islamic heritage while Pakistan would include almost the whole of the Indus Valley, the seat of the earliest civilization in the subcontinent. Historical monuments and museum exhibits were divided up on a territorial basis. However, those objects that were on loan and caught on the *wrong* side of the border on 15 August 1947 created complications. The Council declared that all objects that had been removed for temporary display after 1 January 1947 would be returned to the original museums. Twelve thousand odd objects from Mohenjo-Daro on display in Delhi became a bone of contention between India and Pakistan. The solution, in keeping with the illogic of the Partition, was to divide up the collection, even if it meant breaking up some of these artefacts. History was to be partitioned at the expense of its integrity and preservation (Lahiri 2012).

The situation was even more complicated when it came to government employees and army personnel. In the case of such employees of British India, the Partition Council decided to give them the option to serve either the Government of India or the Government of Pakistan. The general assumption was that religion would be the guiding force in enabling the employees to choose their respective governments. Recognizing that such decisions needed time, the Council allowed for a provisional decision to be valid for six months. For those Hindus, Muslims, and Sikhs who would become minority civil servants, the choice was often between serving the state and serving the nation. Often their decisions were made not only owing to the insecurities of their domestic environments but also because of coercion from their neighbours and co-workers. Despite the efforts to divide government personnel in an organized manner, the situation was complicated as many sought to change their 'options' depending on the chances of a quick promotion, marital and family status, and judgements about personal safety in a rapidly volatile political climate (Roy 2012).

Religion and its connections to national loyalty mattered the most when it came to dividing the armed forces. The Council's mandate was to divide up the regiments based on their religious composition with the caveat that a Muslim soldier from Pakistan would not be able to opt for the Indian army and a non-Muslim soldier from India would not be able to join the Pakistani army. Such a method kept the system of unit class composition intact; only individual officers and minority units had the right to declare for either country. Most regiments in the Indian army had a fixed composition before 1947, which meant that at the time of the Partition, the overall Hindu, Muslim, or Sikh proportion of a regiment determined where it would get allotted. Thus, 8 infantry regiments with 50–75 per cent Muslims went to Pakistan and the remaining 18 regiments were allotted to India. Minorities within these majority units would then be transferred out. The number at this level of exchange did not match and some regiments grew bigger and some smaller (Wilkinson 2015). Such an orderly directive belies the confusion in the minds of the soldiers who were being exchanged. For example, the Hindustani Muslims of the PAVO Cavalry, although assigned to Pakistan, opted initially to join India but then decided only later to join Pakistan (Effendi 2007).

The nearly half-a-million-strong British Indian army was divided along religious lines precisely at the time when a united, neutral army could have been used to suppress some of the Partition-generated violence in northern India. The armed forces had mostly mixed regiments barring a few, and men of various castes and religious affiliations had lived and fought side by side. While some of these regiments had been generally immune to the nationalistic fervour and communal allegiances in the 1940s, other regiments were heavily politicized. But on the eve of the Partition, soldiers were labelled Indian or Pakistani and many of them started to openly identify with these markers. Critical to such fashioning was the problematic equivalence drawn between Muslim soldiers and Pakistan and non-Muslim soldiers and India, irrespective of whether or not they themselves supported these new states.

Moreover, Punjab, which had been the traditional recruiting ground of the British army, witnessed the desertion of large numbers of soldiers who went to join militias as news of violence in their hometowns filtered in (Khan 2007). Consequently, the reliable manpower available to cover large areas engulfed in the chaos was shockingly thin. The contradictory efforts embedded within the Partition process—to divide the army equitably and prevent a civil war—made the chances of success improbable.

Borders and Boundaries

Faced with the reality of an impending division, the focus of how to effect partition shifted to claims on land based on population ratios. The ambiguity of the demand for Pakistan and the Congress's claims of a subcontinental nation now had to meet the reality of definite coordinates. The Plan mandated that the partition of territory would involve the demarcation of new 'boundaries on the basis of ascertaining the contiguous majority areas of Muslims and non-Muslims and in doing so take into account also other factors' (Mansergh et al. 1983). Where a clear continuity of demographic majority became difficult to establish, the 'other factors' would assume primacy. The terms of reference were simple and vague, leading to further questions: What would be the basic unit to determine contiguity? What would and could be 'other factors'? What weightage would each of the terms—'demography', 'contiguous areas', and 'other factors'—have in relation to each other? What was clear was that religious demography would be key, and very quickly people were reduced to numerical units based on religion in calculations of population ratios. The historical and present reality of mixed communities and interwoven lives were pushed aside in these claims and counterclaims of prospective national territories.

Mountbatten appointed a Boundary Commission under the chairmanship of Sir Cyril Radcliffe to delineate the new boundaries in a timely and orderly manner. Divided into two regional Boundary Commissions with four members each (two Hindu and two Muslim), it was tasked with deciding the boundaries in Bengal and Punjab. In keeping with the rational facade of the work of the Commission, the members were all well-known judges. Radcliffe had the deciding vote within each of these commissions.

The task of the Boundary Commission was an impossible one for many reasons. The Commission had less than six weeks to decide the lines of partition in both the east and the west. Further, the absence of updated maps, field surveys, credible census numbers, and the lack of time for input of knowledge from local administrators severely hampered the process. Further, the deliberations were done in an atmosphere of hostility and distrust. Thus, when Radcliffe suggested that it would be less disruptive if India and Pakistan jointly operated the headworks of Punjab's complex canal system, Jinnah reportedly responded that he would rather have deserts in Pakistan than fertile lands that depended on water from the Hindus. Nehru was equally reluctant to share and informed Radcliffe that India's rivers and the decisions on how to use them were India's affair (Chester 2009; Gilmartin 2015).

The appointment of Cyril Radcliffe was itself problematic. He had no experience either with the processes of boundary-making or with India. Oddly enough, in British eyes, such lack of experience made him impartial. However, instead of being objective, Radcliffe's bias towards maintaining British interests impelled him to ensure that the Commission and its verdict had a facade of rational deliberations rather than the appearance of a hurried outcome. Scholars differentially highlight how much influence and agency Indians, both leaders and the public, had over the deliberations that would lead to the new borders. Some argue that Indian politicians gave little thought to how the new lines would affect minority groups, the physical infrastructure, or the economic activities at what would become border zones (Chatterji 1999;

Schendel 2005). Others point to the British to suggest that what was at stake for the British was the perception of control and of being in charge of the decolonization process. Thus, the fact that there was little room to manoeuvre within a religiously determined mandate and the problematic structure of the commissions, which predictably led to deadlocks that only Radcliffe could and would unlock, predicated the award of the Boundary Commission (Chester 2009).

The lack of cooperation at the top was coupled with total confusion at the popular level. Even though the Boundary Commission did not solicit the opinions of the people, and there was little time for it, individuals and civic and political groups in Bengal and Punjab wrote letters and petitions of their own volition in the hope of ensuring the *right* delineation of the border. Civic organizations were set up for this very purpose and a range of arguments based on census data, self-drawn geographical and geological maps, and historical and religious connections comprised such claims of inclusion (Roy 2012).

The Bengal Boundary Commission met behind closed doors in Calcutta in the last weeks of July 1947. The League and a joint coalition of the Congress, the Hindu Mahasabha, and others presented their arguments for maximum territory. There were two main bones of contention between the League and the Congress advocates: first, while the League wanted the basic unit of the Partition to be a subdivision, which they argued would make for a less complicated boundary, the Congress lobbied for the *thana*, the area under the jurisdiction of one police station, to be the basic unit of enumeration. Both arguments would provide greater territories to the respective claimants.

Second, the League insisted that the principle of contiguity should be limited to the areas within the province of Bengal. This meant that if an area was contiguous to other non-Muslim majority areas in India but not contiguous to any such areas within Bengal, then it should automatically go to Pakistan. This argument could then be used to include non-Muslim majority districts of the Chittagong Hill Tracts, Jalpaiguri, and Darjeeling in Pakistan. The city of Calcutta was central to the arguments put forward by both parties. Here the clause of 'other factors' was used innovatively as the League argued that despite its majority non-Muslim population, the city's economic and commercial significance as a major port and centre of jute production should be the guiding factors.

In addition, the Congress coalition demanded that the division should entail the maximum number of non-Muslims in West Bengal and Muslims in East Bengal. This would ensure that the proportion of Muslims in East Bengal to the total Muslim population of the province would not be unduly higher or lower than the proportion of non-Muslims in West Bengal to the entire non-Muslim population of the province. Such religious balance between non-Muslims and Muslims, in the minds of these leaders, would prevent any migration of minorities in divided Bengal.

In the end, the award in Bengal followed closely with the Congress's demands. It assigned 36.36 per cent of the land to accommodate 35.14 per cent of the population to West Bengal while East Bengal/Pakistan received 63.6 per cent of the land and 64.85 per cent of the population. Consequently, the two states had an equal proportion of majority and minority populations in a ratio of approximately 70:30. The award was inequitable in its distribution of minority population as 16 per cent of the total Muslim population of Bengal remained in the west while East Bengal/ Pakistan retained 42 per cent of the total non-Muslim population.

The boundary divided the five districts of Nadia, Jessore, Dinajpur, Jalpaiguri, and Malda. The Muslim-majority district of Murshidabad was awarded to India in an effort to keep intact the Hooghly river system. The Commission awarded non-contiguous portions of Darjeeling and Jalpaiguri to West Bengal and counterweighed such decisions by awarding the non-Muslim majority region of Chittagong Hill Tracts to East Pakistan. As the Congress demanded, Calcutta remained part of West Bengal. The new border had to deal with the boundaries of the two princely states of Cooch Behar and Tripura, both of which acceded to India by 1950. However, Radcliffe's patchwork border remained mired in controversy, especially when it came to the issue of enclave territories, which were remnants from Bengal's Mughal past. After 1947, India had 130 enclaves within East Pakistan, and Pakistan claimed 95 enclaves within the Indian territory.

The Punjab Boundary Commission was tasked with dividing Punjab and had to take into consideration 'other factors'. Like the Bengal Boundary Commission, its sessions in Lahore in the last week of July were met with intense lobbying from the major political parties. Eminent lawyers, Motilal C. Setalvad and Sir Zaffarullah Khan, led the Congress and the League delegations respectively. In addition, an Australian geographer, Oskar Spate, was brought in to make a case for the border district of Gurdaspur, which was the seat of the heterodox Ahmadi community. The claims of the Sikhs, in addition to those of the Hindus and Muslims, made the deliberations of the Punjab Commission more complicated. While the claims and counterclaims of each community were divergent and competing, the arguments reflect the push for maximum benefits and greater territories for their own side.

The League based its arguments primarily on the basis of demography, urging that all Muslim-majority districts in Lahore, Rawalpindi, and Multan divisions should be part of Pakistan. In addition, the *tehsil* (subdivision of a district) should be the basic unit to determine contiguous majority areas. In contrast, the Congress's claims were based on 'other factors'. Through the determination of factors such as economic considerations, historical attachments, or disruption of natural boundaries, the Congress case tried to push the boundary as far west as possible. Such arguments went far beyond the actual demographic composition of a particular region. Thus, Lahore was claimed for India because of its historical association with Hindus and Sikhs. Similarly, the Congress claimed Gurdaspur, a Muslim-majority district, not only because its inclusion would preserve a whole network of communications and railways but also because non-Muslims controlled the district's economic interests.

On their part, the Sikhs who had been advocates of a partition in the wake of communal violence in 1946 now submitted a lengthy memorandum urging for the inclusion of Muslim-majority districts such as Lyallpur, Gujranwala, and Sialkot. They argued that these areas were integral to the Sikh identity, as the home of historical and religious sites, and any partition that did not include such areas would be detrimental to the community's economic and cultural integrity. The governor's office was flooded with calls from Sikh representatives who asked that Guru Nanak's birthplace be included in East Punjab and that arrangements be made to transfer Sikhs from Western Punjab to the east (Khan 2007). However, the Sikhs were told that there was little that the outgoing British administration could do and that they would have to wait for the decisions of the Boundary Commission.

In Punjab, the Radcliffe Award allotted approximately 62 per cent of the area of undivided Punjab to India. Consequently, 55 per cent of the population found themselves in India. The border began from the edge of Kashmir south along the Ujh River, leaving one tehsil of Gurdaspur to Pakistan and awarding the rest of the district to India. It divided the Lahore district on the demographic majority at the tehsil level and allowed 'other factors' to suppress the dictates of a communal majority. In contrast, the Amritsar district, which had a bare majority of non-Muslims, was allotted entirely to India. The allocation of a major part of Gurdaspur (with its bare majority of Muslims) remains controversial to this day. It is generally understood that such an award was done to provide India with access to Jammu and Kashmir. The line ended at the border of Bhawalpur, a princely state whose ruler later acceded to Pakistan. In addition to creating large enclaves of minority populations who were displaced and uprooted, the Radcliffe Award significantly disrupted the canal network and damaged the integrity of the province's irrigation system. Two of the province's canal headworks were now in India, although the bulk of the areas irrigated by the canals lay in Pakistan (Chester 2009).

Although the Radcliffe Award was ready by 12 August, Mountbatten, fearing the inevitable civil strife once the border became known, arranged for its announcement only on 17 August, two days after India and Pakistan came into being, when the British had officially relinquished constitutional control over their empire. The award failed to satisfy anyone, and engendered confusion and a sense of betrayal among Hindus and Muslims. Press comments after the announcement characterized it as 'a departing kick of British imperialism' (*Amrita Bazar Patrika*) and 'territorial murder' (*Dawn*) (Roy 2012). Controversies over the allotment of Gurdaspur, Ferozepore's allocation to India, and Khulna's allocation to East Pakistan were quick to emerge in the public mind, as Radcliffe became the poster child of British bias.

There were several peculiar features of the new international borders. East and West Pakistan were separated by over a thousand miles, even though constitutionally they were one nation state. While the border between India and West Pakistan was closed to travel within a couple of years and would become highly surveilled by India and Pakistan, the border between India and East Pakistan would remain open for travel until 1952. The lines themselves, both in divided Punjab and Bengal, cut haphazardly through agricultural lands, dividing villages from their markets, through river systems and dense jungles that were difficult to delineate and defend, and sometimes through individual houses, dividing the bedroom from the living room. The border divided families, communities from their sacred pilgrimage sites, farmers from their plots of land, and workers from their factories.

In their efforts to divide the assets and land, very few officials considered the impact of such a separation on the people. There was little attention paid to warnings of mass exodus or the potential for large-scale violence. Most significantly, the border was perceived to be the dividing line between 'us' and 'them' and between 'our territory' and 'foreign territory'. Consequently, its announcement and the inadequacy of the Punjab Boundary Force in maintaining law and order quickly escalated the atmosphere of fear and insecurity into horrific communal violence. Individuals and communities who were caught on the 'wrong' side of the border now fought to reverse the line. The communal logic of the Partition, which had depended on religious demographic calculations, now manifested itself in community efforts to drive out and erase opposing communities and stake out claims of one nation over the other.

Structures of Violence

As the deliberations of the Partition Council and the Boundary Commission brought the reality of the impending partition closer, violence between communities erupted in several places in Punjab and northern India. Such violence had actually already begun the year before with the Great Calcutta Killings in August 1946 and continued in fits and starts until the mid-1950s. Partition violence, defined by its extent and brutality, is central to our understanding of the division in 1947. It spared no one. Involving not only the men, women, and children of the warring communities, it impacted non-members who resided in the areas engulfed in violence.

While there was significant variation in the form, extent, and immediate responsibility of communal rioting between 1946 and 1950, what is clear is that such riots were qualitatively different from previous clashes. At one level, the horrors of Partition violence were retributive at their core, and ebbed and flowed with tales of atrocities and images of trains arriving with dead bodies of passengers (Brass 2003). Individual rioters were often motivated by the desire of loot or women and found their actions to be socially sanctioned in an atmosphere of communal animosity. Complicity and tacit support of neighbours and those who were responsible for preventing such atrocities needs to be taken into account (Khan 2007). Partition violence was also linked to the fast-paced political developments and accentuated by an atmosphere of increasing distrust and fear. Deliberate propaganda identifying potential perpetrators and victims played a crucial role in exacerbating the already communalized environment.

At another level, the extent and the brutality of the violence is partly explained by the presence of recently demobilized ex-soldiers of the British Indian army who not only had combat experience but were able to train paramilitary and volunteer groups as well as provide them with access to arms and ammunition (Aiyar 1998). The methodical attempt to wipe out entire neighbourhoods and populations depended largely on the actions of volunteer groups such as the Sikh Jathas and Muslim war tribal parties. Attacks on refugees on foot, convoys, and refugee trains that were frequently made with military precision indicate the complicity of railway officials with such groups.

Partition violence was also different because perpetrators could easily mark out their communal enemies, and violence often escalated rapidly and widely, revealing that such events were planned actions rather than spontaneous eruptions. In fact, the nature of Partition-related violence shows dimensions of 'ethnic cleansing' as rival communities sought to harm, kill, and displace opposing communities in ways that prevented any possibility of reconstitution at the end of the violent confrontations (Copeland 1998). Thus, not only were individuals targeted but also their families and their homes; their businesses were razed to the ground. The repertoire of violence between the communities on all sides included profaning everything that was of sacred and symbolic value to the other side—from pigs and cows slain in front of mosques and temples to the circumcision of non-Muslim men, from the forced conversions and consumption of beef by Hindus to the sexual violation of women belonging to the 'enemy'— nothing was off limits.

The exact numbers of people killed is difficult to estimate given that the killings happened over a period of two to four years during an administrative breakdown when the reporting and recording of deaths was not a priority for anyone. Most scholars, using census figures, contemporary press reports, and eyewitness accounts, provide a range between 200,000 and 2 million (Menon and Bhasin 1998; Butalia 1998). Most scholars now accept that approximately 1 million people died from Partition-related violence. As an estimate, this number cannot be broken down in terms of community and gender of the dead. Beyond numbers, what is more significant is the nature of violence that marked minorities and majorities, created victims and perpetrators within communities and families, and the immensity of human suffering amplified by the lack of official support to reduce the violence and provide safety and security to their new citizens.

Women, as Gandhi described them in the context of the Partition, were the 'chief sufferers' as they faced violence from men of other communities, their own family members, and their nations. Partition-related brutality targeting women and children brought violence within the domestic sphere for the first time. Around 75,000 women belonging to different communities were abducted and raped by men belonging to another community (and sometimes their own). Sometimes, women had their breasts cut off, their genitalia mutilated, and were branded with symbols of the other community. They were sometimes paraded naked as a show of power for the perpetrators and to shame their community. Such violence sought to mark women's bodies as representations of their community and family honour (Butalia 1998).

Familiar forms of sexual violence were now charged with symbolic meaning and used not only to violate female bodies 'belonging' to the other community, but also as representations of territory that could be conquered and dishonoured. Consequently, women's bodies were inscribed with religious iconography and nationalist slogans—'Pakistan Zindabad' and 'Jai Hind'. Rape as a tool of communal violence and shaming had been popular in the riots in eastern India in 1946 and became ubiquitous in the context of retributive violence in Punjab. Many women faced violence from their own family members as they were forced to commit suicide in order to pre-empt any sexual violence against them and to preserve their chastity and protect individual family and community honour. Their choices included poisoning themselves, jumping into wells, and/or setting themselves ablaze (Butalia 1998).

In addition to physical violence, women of both communities were often taken as hostages, and many were forced to become wives and companions of their captors. Official figures put about 50,000 such Muslim women in India and 33,000 Hindu and Sikh women in Pakistan. In the aftermath of the Partition, both India and Pakistan engaged in the 'recovery' of these women and were more concerned with the numbers recovered than the women's wishes. Consequently, those who had made peace with the violence and their captors were once again uprooted, forced to part with

79

their children from such alliances, and returned to their 'home' countries without much thought given to their future or social acceptance in the still communalized climate of the 1950s (Menon and Bhasin 1998).

The understandings of the nature of Partition violence have primarily been framed by what happened in Punjab and by the pre-Partition riots in eastern India. These focus on large-scale violence that involved physical maiming and killing of great numbers of people. However, Partition violence was also routine, small-scale, and individualized, targeting victims through sporadic stabbings, lootings, and destruction of properties. Significantly, such violence, in West Bengal and East Pakistan, threatened the psyche rather than the body and was mediated by petty theft, loot, kidnapping, destruction and defacement of religious icons, verbal threats, and rumours. Together, they created an environment of fear and insecurity that was embellished by political rhetoric and thinly veiled state propaganda. Such routine violence engendered the attrition of traditional ties and often minority families, fearful of potential violence, were forced to leave their homes to seek security across the border (Roy 2012).

The cycle of Partition-related violence began on 16 August, the day when the League called for 'Direct Action'. The day was to mark the formal push towards the achievement of Pakistan through nationwide *hartal*s (stoppage of work as sign of mourning or political protest) and demonstrations. In Calcutta, the League ministry under Suhrawardy declared 16 August a holiday and plans had been made to hold a huge public rally. The government also promised that there would be no police interference at the rally. However, as one eyewitness later reminisced, it was 'going to be unlike all other days' (Bourke-White, quoted in Banerjee-Dube 2015). On its way home that afternoon, the peaceful rally turned, it would seem, spontaneously insane as it attacked Hindus and looted homes and property. The Hindu counter-attack was swift and the carnage on both sides continued until 20 August, killing around 4,000 and injuring 10,000 others. Margaret Bourke-White, the American photojournalist, captured the horrors in frames showing vultures waiting on rooftops to feast on the dead lying in the streets. Having witnessed the atrocities of the Nazi concentration camps a year earlier, she noted that the streets of Calcutta were similar to those in Buchenwald.

The lack of police action to stop the rioting and the scale at which it erupted have led many scholars to argue that this violence was not only politically motivated but also evidenced some form of premeditation by those at the helm (Das 1991). While the immediate unfolding of events shows the lack of official efforts at curbing the violence, the long-term grievances, communalizing activities of the League and the Hindu Mahasabha, the experience of death and relief during the recent famine, and wartime exigencies and their impact contributed to the monumental scale of violence and communal enmity.

Shortly after the Great Calcutta Killings, riots began in Bombay in early September, followed by Noakhali and Bihar in October, Garmukteswar in the UP in November, and the NWFP in December before engulfing the whole of Punjab by March 1947. While the deaths resulting from sporadic violence in Bombay were limited to a few hundred, in Noakhali, which had a history of Muslim peasant unrest against Hindu landlords and traders, the violence manifested itself through rape, forcible conversions, and destruction of property, resulting in the death of thousands of Hindus. Rather than being spontaneous, the violence was marked by clear strategic organization and the reworking of earlier political and class alliances into strictly basic religious allegiances (Sarkar 1983). Gandhi arrived in Noakhali in the early days of November and remained there until March 1947 to work towards ameliorating the violence and to bring peace in the region.

Gandhi's arrival in Noakhali did much to curb the violence there, but the violence managed to spread to Bihar where thousands of Muslims were killed and injured and many more were displaced. In Bihar, the violence broke the urban–rural divide, affecting equally both the urban centres and rural countryside in Patna, Gaya, Bhagalpur, and Monghyr (Munger). In November, violence began at a local religious fair in the town of Garmukteswar, in the Meerut district. Around 350 people were killed, properties and businesses were destroyed, and several girls were abducted. Like the rioting in previous months, here, too, one observes the well-planned and organized nature. In this case, RSS members had marked all the Muslim shops that were attacked and burnt without much damage to the neighbouring Hindu shops (Khan 2007).

The province that experienced the core of the violence was Punjab where, beginning in March 1947, Hindus, Muslims, and Sikhs attacked and killed each other. Communal tensions intensified when the Unionist Ministry in Punjab, with British support, banned the Muslim National Guard and the RSS in January 1947. The consequent civil disobedience movement organized by the League resulted in the resignation of the coalition government of the Unionist Party on 2 March. During a protest demonstration in front of the Assembly Chamber organized by the Sikh leadership, Master Tara Singh unsheathed his sword, provoking extreme interpretations in the popular mind (Khan 2007). The violence engulfing the cities of Lahore and Amritsar was immediately followed by riots in Multan, Attock, and Rawalpindi as Muslims destroyed Hindu and Sikh properties. The violence quickly escalated to killings as entire villages were destroyed, corpses of children were hung from trees, and young girls were raped. By August 1947, over 5,000 people had been killed in Punjab. The lack of accountability and punishment of the perpetrators in Punjab indicated that the region was just getting started on its path to a communal inferno.

Violence in Punjab and northern India got a new life in the month of August, especially around the time of Independence and the announcement of the Boundary Award. As Hindu, Sikh, and Muslim refugees began moving across the new borders, violence erupted between them along zones of crossing, in trains carrying them, and in neighbourhoods that had been emptied of residents and filled with the displaced. The latter was particularly true for Delhi, which, by September 1947, had experienced the kind of horrific violence that had previously engulfed Punjab. Hindu and Sikh refugees arriving from West Punjab targeted Muslim residents of the city and the resulting violence led to the death of around 20,000 Muslims. By 1951, nearly 330,000 Muslims had left Delhi. Most of them took up residence in Karachi, dramatically changing the culture and demography of the city. Violence linked to the initial arrival of the refugees in Karachi began in January 1948, leaving around 200 dead and over 10,000 Hindu residents in refugee camps waiting for evacuation to India. In the case of both Delhi and Karachi, the violence was not only retributive, but was also the consequence of routine violence that sought to make space for the incoming population amidst housing shortages (Zamindar 2007).

Partition violence spilled beyond the boundaries of Punjab into the princely states of Alwar, Bharatpur, and in Jammu and Kashmir where tens of thousands were killed between 1947 and 1948. In Alwar and Bharatpur, the princes used their state forces to target violence against the ethnic Muslim group, the Meos, killing nearly 30,000 and forcing another 100,000 to flee (Mayaram 1997).

The cycle of violence continued in Punjab and northern India until the middle of 1949, but saw its last flicker in eastern India and East Pakistan. The riots of 1950 that began as a communist insurrection were quickly transformed into mimetic communal riots in Dacca, Khulna, Barisal, and Sylhet in East Pakistan, and Assam, Calcutta, and the border districts of Nadia, Murshidabad, and Cooch Behar in India. Significantly, the violence that exhibited the breach between Hindus and Muslims did not differentiate between class and caste identity (Roy 2012). Scheduled Castes and Santhal sharecroppers, who had been active in the Tebhaga Movement (rural agrarian protests led by the Communist Party in 1946–7 in Bengal around the demand of three-fourths share for peasants) in previous years, found themselves included as 'non-Muslims' within instances of clearly defined communal violence (Bandyopadhyay 2004). Similar to Punjab, non-Muslims in East Pakistan saw forced conversions, their properties looted, villages burnt, and places of worship desecrated. In India, Muslims faced similar violence and refugees poured into East Pakistan. These riots, although the last of the specifically Partition-related communal eruptions, engendered the largest cross-border migration in divided Bengal.

Not everyone experienced Partition violence and the 'August anarchy' (Aiyar 1998) did not affect every region of northern India that had mixed communities. In the small Muslim-ruled state of Malerkotla, located in central Punjab, no one died and it is remembered as the community's finest hour. Here, the myths surrounding its founding Sufi saint, Haidar Shaikh, the fact that its history included it being blessed by one of the Sikh gurus, Guru Gobind Singh, and, most importantly, having a ruler willing to deploy force to stop any violence, combined to create an 'oasis of peace' (Bigelow 2009). Again, eastern India, which had experienced the first throes of Partition violence, remained relatively calm in 1947–9. Gandhi's moral imperative to keep peace between communities also helped in calming things down in Calcutta in 1946, and then again in Noakhali. Gandhi's fasts to end communal enmity together with his advocacy for non-violence in a very violent time had some impact in stalling the riots in the areas where he was physically present.

Many followed Gandhi's example and carried out heroic and humanitarian acts even in such horrific times. There are numerous personal and eyewitness narratives of Hindus helping Muslims and vice-versa during the violence, hiding them from rioters, protecting properties and women belonging to the other community. Qurratulain Haidar, who fled from Dehradun with her mother to Karachi, Pakistan, remembers being hidden under a quilt by three American women missionaries from an angry Hindu mob looking for Muslim victims (Whitehead 1996). Peace demonstrations were held by civic organizations urging for Hindu–Muslim unity and 'communal harmony' days were observed in cities that were experiencing violence.

Differences in class, social status, caste, and gender impacted how Partition violence was experienced. In Lahore, Amritsar, Delhi, and Calcutta, violence was concentrated on certain working-class neighbourhoods while the elites in these cities went about their business as usual. Class and access to resources affected how one could escape violence by possessing the ability to move quickly from one country to another by air or personal vehicles rather than by trains or foot columns (Kaur 2007). Being a Dalit at the time of Partition meant their marginality and invisibility within Hindu society now rendered them 'invisible' to Partition violence. However, their status as menial workers meant that their absence was felt in civic life as both India and Pakistan devised policies to retain their Dalit citizens (Butalia 1998; Pandey 2001).

While official reports indicate that neither the Congress nor the Muslim League anticipated the horrific cycles of violence, much of the 'unthinkability' of the violence and the bafflement of contemporaries indicates—as one scholar puts it—'the systematic disconnect between popular and elite constructions of territory, nationalism and nationality' (Naqvi 2008). Partition violence consequently bordered on ethnic cleansing and achieved a far greater demographic division than anticipated; transforming Amritsar, for example, from a Muslim-majority city before the Partition to one that had no Muslim residents after 1947. Similarly, Lahore's traditional mixed demographic of Hindu, Muslim, and Sikhs changed as Muslims became the dominant population after the Partition. In eastern India, the story was different, partly owing to the lack of large-scale violence during 1947. While there was large-scale migration of Hindus from East Pakistan and Muslims from eastern India, many continued to remain as minority residents in their traditional homelands.

The impossibility of the task of dividing territories and populations is brought out poignantly by one of the greatest contemporary storytellers of the Partition, Saadat Hasan Manto, who lamented, 'I sat down to write but found my thoughts scattered. Despite my best efforts I could not dissociate India from Pakistan and Pakistan from India' (Manto 2008).

3

Refugees, Citizens, and the Making of the Nation

The creation of India and Pakistan was a testament to national belonging as Hindus, Sikhs, and Muslims caught in the 'wrong' state were forced to seek refuge in the 'right' state, leaving their homes as well as their traditional social and cultural bonds behind. The ongoing violence and the environment of fear and insecurity regarding the potential status of those who were deemed minorities were central to engendering the largest forced migration of the twentieth century. Such movement changed the demographic characters of entire cities such as Lahore, Amritsar, and Dacca. Managing and providing relief and rehabilitation to such 'people on the move' took up much of the energies of the new states and were also key to how India and Pakistan framed themselves.

The tides of people flowing out of India and Pakistan were unbelievable and, until August of 1947, unthinkable. In the course of four years between 1947 and 1951, recent scholarship estimates that around 14.5 million people moved between India, West Pakistan, and East Pakistan, and an additional 3.7 million were 'missing' or dead (Bharadwaj, Khwaja, and Mian 2008). In these years, the pace of migration was swifter and greater on the border between India and West Pakistan, and was a two-way process that petered out by the end of 1949. In contrast, migration in eastern India had begun in the wake of the riots of 1946, and, although things remained relatively calm during the days leading up to the Partition and after, migration, especially of Hindus from East Bengal to West Bengal, Assam, and Tripura, continued steadily. The riots of 1950 engendered the highest numbers of post-Partition migration, which was a two-way movement in that minority Muslims from Bihar and West Bengal moved to East Pakistan in addition to the continued movement of Hindus into India. The migration across the eastern border lasted nearly two decades after the Partition and was characterized by its chronic intensity. In this time frame, at least 6 million Hindus crossed into India and 1.5 million Muslims left India for East Pakistan.

People moved in various ways depending on their access to resources. Thus while air travel was common, it was limited to the rich and privileged. More common were trains, crammed to the maximum, an image that remains central to our image of the movement of people. In addition, travel by steamers and boats was popular, especially across the Bengal delta, carrying people from parts of rural East Bengal to points in India, and crossing the Arabian Sea was popular in moving people from Bombay to Karachi and vice-versa. People also travelled on foot, in large columns and *kafila*s (caravan or foot column), taking only what they could carry. These foot columns were sometimes 30,000–40,000 strong, creating caravans that were 45 miles long. The time and distance were also massive, sometimes taking migrants over 3 weeks to reach their destination and traversing over 400 miles. The swiftness with which one could travel often influenced the level of violence one would have to encounter. Foot columns going in opposite directions would often attack each other or be attacked by residents in the area they were passing through.

Initially, India and Pakistan were completely unprepared to tackle the Partition 'refugee crisis'. Often improvised, early relief efforts operated from the party headquarters of the Congress and the League where workers were often dependent on the resources and goodwill of volunteers. By the end of September, both countries launched extensive relief operations and established ministries to deal exclusively with the crisis. Given the nature of migration and the fact that the needs of the refugees were localized, it was difficult to come up with a 'catch-all' solution to the crisis. However, Partition refugees and their rehabilitation was framed as a 'national problem' in both countries and helped strengthen their respective political centralization and augment their executive powers (Chatterji 2007; Zamindar 2007).

Rethinking Partition Migration

Our understanding of Partition migration needs to counter certain common perceptions. First, the migration of Hindus, Sikhs, and Muslims was not a simple 'exchange' of population. In fact, no one and none of the plans for Partition included or anticipated such fallout. The Plan anticipated that minority communities in each state would be balancing safeguards offering protection against violence from their majority communities, and such a communal détente would ensure peace. Even in September 1947, at the height of Partition migration, Jinnah repeatedly tried to assure Pakistan's non-Muslim residents that they would be 'free to go to your temples … or to any other place of worship in this state of Pakistan'. Similarly, Nehru stressed that India was the land for all

Indians and that Muslims in India would have the same rights of citizenship as anyone else.

Such promises to safeguard minority rights, amidst the ongoing violence, uprooting, and the breakdown of bureaucratic infrastructure, came too late and were not enough to assuage fears and uncertainties. The consequent migration/relocation was often not intended to be permanent as many people moved across the border conditionally with plans to return home once things became normal. However, the subsequent years witnessed that any attempt to return was made extremely difficult by the passage of legislations and bureaucratic actions in India and Pakistan, who sought to control and regulate movement on their mutual borders.

A rethinking of Partition migration also needs to take into account the difference in attitude of the Indian state towards the movement of people across its eastern and western borders. The reality of violence on the western border quickly led the Indian government to adopt a policy of evacuating Punjabi minorities with the help of the army. In contrast, such an 'exchange of population' was deemed unnecessary on the Bengal frontier and Nehru noted that 'the business of shifting millions of people is beyond our capacity'. Consequently, in Bengal, the Indian government took measures to ensure the safety and security of minorities through bilateral negotiations with the Pakistani government and discouraged any exodus. Such efforts failed and contributed to the chronic and continued nature of the migrations in this region.

Partition's migrants comprised of people beyond the Hindu, Muslim, and Sikh communities and impacted demographic changes beyond divided Bengal and Punjab. Christians, Dalits, and Parsees, identified as 'non-Muslims', were often part of the Partition migrations. While Dalits in West Bengal were both perpetrators and victims of violence, in Punjab, Dalits were largely excluded from the arc of violence. However, this does not mean that the Dalit communities remained untouched by the Partition. Many migrated to the other side under the threat of conversion or in search of better opportunities. In Western Punjab, and in Sind, the departure of Dalits, who had traditionally performed important but menial sanitation services, quickly impacted those regions. In eastern India, the Namasudras began to migrate after 1950 from East Pakistan to escape both the violence targeting them and economic deprivation.

Recent scholarship has suggested that the Dalits in Punjab were 'nobody's people', meaning that neither India nor Pakistan spoke for them the way they spoke for the three dominant religious communities (Pandey 2001). On the other hand, as a community, they became important to both nation states: Pakistan wanted to retain them to ensure access to traditional menial labour, while India wanted them to migrate to India as evidence of the Pakistani state's inability to guarantee their safety and security. Consequently, a generally marginalized community became nationalized. Parsees and Christians, on the other hand, had no special identity in terms of their work. Anglo-Indians were perceived to be close to the British and occupied an ambiguous space within the Partition's demographic stratosphere. They often migrated out of both India and Pakistan to destinations in Britain and its Commonwealth.

People moved from the epicentres of violence in Bengal and Punjab as well as areas that had remained untouched or had little experience of Partition violence. Thus, Hindus from Sindh moved to Gujarat in the wake of the Partition but had very little experience of bloodshed and violence. The insecurities and the uncertainties of the Partition influenced other Hindus from the NWFP and Muslims from Bombay and Bihar to cross the borders in search of safety and security. Migrants often moved to places closer to the border and found it useful to move to places that had been vacated by other migrants moving in the opposite direction or to cities such as Lahore, Delhi, and Calcutta where rehabilitative economic prospects were better. In a lot of these cases, such uprooting was a temporary, precautionary measure in the face of violence or its potential and people intended to return to their homes once things calmed down. However, as we shall see, new documentary, evacuation, and relief policies made such hopes of return impossible.

One also needs to take into account the multiple reasons why people left. For a majority, especially in the riot-torn areas of Bengal and Punjab, an escape from the horrific violence was the primary reason. In such cases, movement was often unplanned with no specific intention other than that of crossing the border. For others, who had the luxury of being away from the epicentres of violence, the choice of whether to stay or go was often long-drawn-out and tortuous. Bengali Hindu refugees moved chronically into India depending upon changing bilateral ties between India and Pakistan as well as the changing communal context in East Bengal. Often families did not move together, preferring to send daughters and sons away to safety while the parents or the elderly remained to hold on to their homes and properties. For many minorities in the subsequent years, the decision to migrate stemmed from ideological concerns as well as concerns about economic and social discrimination. Thus, many Muslims from northern India migrated to East Pakistan to contribute to the crafting of the new homeland.

Last but not the least, we need to rethink the categories of the Partition's migrants not only along axes of gender, class, caste, and religion, but also in terms of location and time—where they were from and where they went and when they moved. The scholarship on Partition refugees is vast and the Partition refugee has become an important icon of national consciousness through literary and film representations. Numerous studies have focused on the relationship between the refugees, the policies regarding their relief and rehabilitation from the Indian state, and their consequent impact on national and regional politics (Bose 2000; Ansari 2005; Chatterji 2007). Others have focused on refugee voices and how their Partition experiences led to the reframing of their identities in their host societies (Bagchi and Dasgupta 2003; Kaur 2007). Such studies have generally privileged the educated and middle-class narrative in urban centres in divided Punjab and Bengal. In addition, the dominant image of the Partition refugee has been the Punjabi or Sikh refugee arriving in Delhi and its outskirts, and the Bengali Hindu fleeing from East Pakistan to Calcutta. These images tend to assume that all migrants crossed the new borders to be Partition refugees (Schendel 2003).

Only recently has this class and locational bias been fractured and new studies focus on, for example,

Sindhi refugees, those who moved to Tripura and the Andaman Islands, and refugees who moved from parts of India to settle in the borderlands of East Pakistan (Schendel 2005; Kothari 2007; Sen 2014; Cons 2016). Significantly, new scholarship has tended to re-categorize the movement of cross-border settlers—cultivators and women with marital homes on one side and natal homes on the other—and of cross-border labour migrants in search of jobs. A large number of people, especially in the eastern borderlands, left their homes out of fear of persecution and localized violence, but settled in places not far from their homes across the border. These borderland refugees, unlike the archetypal Partition refugees, kept in touch with their relatives and friends who had stayed back (Schendel 2003). In fact, a rethinking of the categories also needs to incorporate the experiences of those who remained in their homes, refusing to let go, and took on the mantle of 'minorities' in India and Pakistan.

Last, the vast movements of people and the official efforts to control, regulate, and count such migration produced a range of terms to describe, sometimes, the same individual. Official terminology in Pakistan identified Muslim refugees from northern India as 'Muhajirs', alluding to the migration of Prophet Mohammed and his disciples from Mecca to Medina in AD 622. Ironically, even though the new Pakistani state actively discouraged migration, such naming was an attempt to ideologically reinforce the idea of Pakistan as a Muslim homeland and imbue a sense of religious significance to the hardships of migration and displacement (Zamindar 2007). India identified its Partition migrants as 'displaced persons' and as 'refugees'. By the 1950s, the term 'refugee' was giving way to 'displaced person' as the Indian state determined that in terms of compensation, a 'displaced person' was not necessarily a 'refugee'. True, that by crossing the border, refugees (and this was more relevant on the eastern front) had fulfilled one of the parameters of refugeehood, that is, displacement. However, the other criterion for recognition of a 'refugee' was the experience of violence or the fear of violence as the cause for such displacement. What constituted violence or the fear of violence was not clearly articulated and remained contingent. In the case of migrants from East Bengal, the preferential use of 'displaced persons' rather than 'refugees' also served to extract any political reason for the migration, and thus to ignore their claims to rehabilitation and subsequent citizenship.

Significantly, the same individuals or groups of individuals could be refugees in one country and 'evacuees' in the other. Muslims from India who left their property behind soon found their properties requisitioned for the rehabilitation of Hindu and Sikh refugees, even while they themselves became refugees in Pakistan. As we shall see, policies regarding the protection of evacuee properties soon ran counter to rehabilitation plans of the new states and made the possibility of return impossible. Migrants, for their part, self-identified in different ways to influence access to relief and rehabilitation and to gain national acceptance as enterprising and resilient citizens of the new states. East Bengali Hindus preferred to see themselves as *udvaastu* (uprooted) or *bastuhara* (without home), indicating their lack of control in their current homelessness. Sindhi Hindus in Gujarat rejected the term 'refugee' for its evocation of helplessness and dependency; instead, they adopted terms such as *purusharthi* (industrious) or *paramarthi* (seeking spiritual salvation) to describe themselves (Kothari 2007).

Refugees and the Republic

By the end of August, both India and Pakistan reversed their initial strategy of trying to stop the migration through verbal assurances and made 'evacuation' their first priority, at least in the case of Punjab. From the very beginning, the Indian state 'partitioned' its policies regarding the migration on the western and eastern frontiers. This differential understanding permeated its border policies and the methods and resources

101

employed to address the refugee rehabilitation, and impacted the post-colonial politics in these regions. Bengal, which had remained relatively calm in 1947, experienced a largely one-way migration from East Pakistan, while both India and Pakistan viewed the migration as unwarranted and to be reversed by continued assurances to their respective insecure minorities. Minority boards were set up to hear grievances, and after the riots of 1950, Nehru and Liaqat Ali, the two premiers, concluded the Delhi Pact, which again made reassurances that minority rights would be guaranteed by the states.

In Punjab, by contrast, the Military Evacuation Organization was formed by September 1947, and refugees began to be transported and airlifted out of makeshift camps to the other side. The 'planned' nature of such state intervention had unplanned consequences as it enabled some local administrators and police to exploit this policy and push out minorities and continue the agenda of ethnic cleansing through dispersal. Thus, in areas of central and western India, Muslim communities were drummed out of India just as Hindus and Sikhs were hounded out of Pakistan (Guha 2008).

In addition to the planned evacuation of the people, both India and Pakistan also agreed to protect the properties of the displaced and manage them until such a time when the displaced returned home. They also agreed not to recognize illegal occupations or seizures of property during the time of Partition. A custodian of evacuee property was established whose jurisdiction included divided Punjab and Delhi, but not the eastern front of Bihar, West Bengal, or Assam, which had significantly similar instances of displacement. The custodian, initially charged with protection of refugee property, very quickly took the view that 'evacuee' property could become the cornerstone of each state's rehabilitation of incoming refugees. Consequently, the activities of the custodian were at cross purposes with the programme of rehabilitation. Such an oppositional relationship made refugee return impossible. In India, the Muslims were the evacuees while Hindus and Sikhs coming from Pakistan were displaced persons who were to be rehabilitated through allotments of evacuee property. As recent scholarship has argued, the departure of Muslim evacuees thus came to be perceived as necessary to accommodate Hindu and Sikh refugees (Zamindar 2007). In Pakistan, a similar process entailed the calculation that needed to equalize the departure of Hindu and Sikh evacuees with the numbers of Muslims from India who could be allowed into Pakistan.

By September 1947, the Indian state formed the Ministry of Rehabilitation, under the leadership of Khitish Chandra Neogy, which created and implemented various relief and rehabilitation policies. The nature and magnitude of relief and rehabilitation operations were unprecedented in scale and range of the tasks at hand. By the end of 1947, there were over a million refugees in West Punjab and over two million in camps in India. The refugee camps dotting the South Asian landscape ranged from vast state-run establishments to small makeshift shelters in schools, temples, mosques, gurdwaras, and public buildings. The largest camp was in Kurukshetra, in East Punjab, which stretched over 9 square miles and was initially planned to accommodate about 100,000 refugees. But in the end, it housed three times that number. While these refugee camps were to be halfway residences on the path to resettle the refugees in different parts of India, many, such as Cooper's camp and the Bijoygarh colony in West Bengal, deliberately transformed themselves into large housing colonies in the subsequent decades.

For both states, centralized planning was seen as a way to resolve the refugee crisis. Both states had a spectrum of tasks at hand that required their immediate attention. First and foremost, officials had to provide the refugees with basic essentials, such as food, clothing, temporary housing, and subsequently materials to restart their lives such as farming equipment, educational and technical training, permanent housing, and agricultural land.

They had to establish and maintain refugee camps in the middle of cities such as Delhi, Karachi, and Calcutta, and in non-urban areas. The Indian government constructed more than half its camps outside Punjab, including 32 in Bombay and 3 in Madras. In addition, it identified areas such as the Andaman Islands and forested lands of Dandyakaranya in Madhya Pradesh where refugees, especially the continuing arrivals from eastern India, could be relocated and rehabilitated.

Most importantly, rehabilitation policies were to ensure that refugees became productive citizens. Thus, the chairman of the Indian Planning Commission argued that for some refugees the Partition could actually be seen as an opportunity of transformation—from being agricultural workers to becoming industrial workers occupied in large public-sector projects envisioned by the new Five-Year Plans. Partition could thus be integrated, at least in official understanding, into the project of nation building.

A large number of middle-class refugees benefitted from government intervention. India and Pakistan paid for the construction of schools and hospitals, sometimes aiding in the creation of new planned localities such as Faridabad and redrawing the urban planning of old cities such as Delhi and Calcutta. In Delhi, Mehr Chand Khanna, the minister of the Public Works Department and Rehabilitation, aimed to provide housing to the refugees and consequently created new colonies in south Delhi such as Lajpat Nagar and Chanakyapuri. Calcutta saw more intervention from refugees themselves as the city limits were extended southwards to incorporate the refugee colonies of Jadavpur and Bijoygarh.

Incoming refugees often arrived with quite different occupational skills and could not or were not qualified to plug the gaps left by those who departed. The State stepped in to retrain such men by imparting technical skills and to train single refugee women and widows in vocational skills such as embroidery and soap making to enable them to be income-earners. Orphans, widows, and any unaccompanied minors were housed in welfare homes and their encounters with the state were imbued with paternalism.

The greatest success in the Indian state's rehabilitation efforts, in a manner of speaking, was the overseeing of land resettlement in divided Punjab and northern India. In Punjab, Hindu and Sikh refugees, who were primarily from agrarian backgrounds, were resettled on land vacated by Muslims in the eastern half of the province as well as in PEPSU (Patiala and East Punjab States Union), Rajasthan, and Delhi. Each family of refugee farmers was initially given a temporary allotment of 4 hectares regardless of what they owned in Pakistan. Loans were advanced to buy farm equipment and seeds. Applications were then invited for permanent allotments that sought greater equivalence with previous land ownership as long as families could provide evidence. By November 1949, nearly 250,000 allotments had been made and the government sought to resettle families with their neighbours as much as possible. The political leadership was able to turn the crisis of the Partition into an opportunity to restructure rural society. Thus, new irrigation projects became part of rehabilitation efforts and led to far-reaching changes that laid the foundations of intensive agriculture. Consequently, by the late 1960s, these would contribute to the emergence of Indian Punjab as the breadbasket of India.

In most cases, rehabilitation efforts were limited by the lack of resources and by policies that refused to pay attention to local contexts and what would work for the refugees in the short and the long term. The cost of relief efforts was massive and created a dent in the new economies; both states spent an estimated 10 million rupees each between 1947 and 1951 and much more in permanent rehabilitation. To add to the crisis, the two new states had to figure out solutions without much help from the international community as Europe focused on post-war reconstructions and its own refugee crisis. International organizations such as the Red Cross declared that the Partition crisis was beyond the scope of its capabilities. The only help came from some Christian missionaries such as the Quakers and the National Christian Council and from some foreign volunteer organizations such as the YMCA (Young Men's Christian Association) and St John's Ambulance, but such help was a mere drop in the ocean (Khan 2007). India and Pakistan also made the decision not to ratify the United Nations Refugee Convention passed in 1951, thereby deliberately ensuring that they alone were responsible for their refugees.

In the domestic front, the divided states and their neighbours were very quickly overstretched in terms of resources and space. However, efforts to disperse refugee populations from these areas met with resistance from other states, which were wary of receiving so many people in the face of food crises and in the cause of maintaining peace. Thus, the UP state government refused to take in refugees in 1947 and attempted to seal its borders. In Gujarat, non-Muslim Sindhis arriving from Pakistan were told that they would not receive any aid. In Assam, the arrival of Bengali refugees created tensions and accentuated demands for ethnic separatism.

Bengal presented the greatest challenge and consequent failure of the rehabilitation efforts of the Indian government. Out of the 18 million people who were uprooted in the wake of the Partition, the largest numbers came from East Bengal. They began arriving in 1947 but continued to arrive chronically in the subsequent two decades. From the start, the Indian state's policies in Bengal aimed not at evacuating minorities, like in Punjab, but at repatriating them through high-level negotiations and meetings promising peace and security in the region. It also viewed the refugees from East Bengal as economic migrants, who were enticed by the Indian state's relief policies. Consequently, the state sought to frame deadlines by which a migrant could officially be deemed a 'refugee' and other deadlines to close down relief and rehabilitation efforts. In accordance with the official view that a Bengali refugee was actually a 'migrant' who could and should return home, the policy in Bengal focused on temporary relief rather than permanent rehabilitation. Between 1947 and 1950, the Indian state thus tried to prevent mass migrations and denied that there was a refugee crisis on the eastern front. However, in the face of continuing refugee movement, the Indian state subsequently shifted the rehabilitation responsibility from the centre to the state.

The continuing exodus of migrants from East Bengal into India, and the Indian state's resistance and inability to recognize the magnitude of the crisis, impacted the efforts towards permanent rehabilitation. In their desire to disperse refugees crowding the stations in Calcutta and squatting in different parts of the city, the Indian state turned a blind eye to refugee preference and regional identity and sought to rehabilitate large groups of Bengali refugees to regions such as Dandyakaranya in Madhya Pradesh and the Andamans. Although large numbers of Bengali refugees were successfully resettled in areas such as Tripura and Uttarakhand, those who were sent to Dandyakaranya faced challenges of language and adversarial reactions from Adivasis who had lived there for generations. Most of the Bengali refugees sent here were peasant Namasudras, who were unfamiliar with the ecology and crop patterns in the area.

The return migration of refugees from Dandyakaranya led to the stereotype embedded in official understanding that the failure of rehabilitation policies in Bengal was owing to the Bengali refugees' lack of enterprise and inherently 'parochial' nature. To make this case more succinct, the 'hard-working' Punjabi refugee, who is seen as self-reliant and resilient, is often brought in for contrast to show the success of the rehabilitation policies in Punjab. Such assertions are, of course, baseless. The contexts of uprooting and the Indian state's rehabilitation policies were strikingly different in Punjab and Bengal. In East Punjab, which had a two-way migration and thus enabled land redistribution, the success of rehabilitation was owing to the state policies being able to harness refugee dynamism into patterns of rehabilitation that harmonized with integrated social development. In contrast, Bengal experienced mostly a one-way migration (except in 1950), which was chronic and long-drawn-out. While Bengali refugees were equally enterprising and creative, their actions were largely directed towards self-rehabilitation in the absence of any matching effort on the part of the Indian state. The failure of rehabilitation in West Bengal was thus a failure of the state.

The Indian state's relief measures were limited in different ways when it came to Dalit and refugee women's access to state-sponsored rehabilitation. More than two million Dalit refugees fled to India between 1947 and 1964, most arriving from East Pakistan into India. However, they remain the 'untouchable' subject in the narrative of the Partition and its migrants, appearing only as numbers to quantify the non-Muslim population. Moreover, as recent scholarship has argued, the Namasudra experiences of displacement and the struggle for rehabilitation in Bengal accentuated their 'Hindu refugee' identity, temporarily overshadowing the ongoing Dalit cultural politics (Sen 2012).

In 1947, there were no separate relief camps for Dalit migrants, although there were some for Muslims. Dalit migrants were housed separately from upper-caste migrants and settled in 'untouchable' housing colonies on the margins of cities such as Delhi. They faced discrimination in terms of rations and in access to state schemes for rehabilitation. Further discrepancies included the grant of compensatory land to only those who had been landowners, but not to those Dalits who had tilled the land. Although such discrimination was not part of the Indian government's state policies, the creation of a separate agency, the Displaced Harijan Rehabilitation Board, to take care of Dalit refugees meant that they were no longer part of the general category. Social reordering engendered by rehabilitation policies thus closely followed prevalent norms of caste distinctions.

In the case of women, both India and Pakistan framed their relief measures in two ways. First, the task at hand was to 'recover and rehabilitate' the thousands of women who had been abducted and remained on both sides of the border. In 1949, the Indian state legislated that non-Muslim women who had been forcibly converted and abducted to Pakistan would be 'recovered' back to their own country. The project to rescue abducted women did not include the repatriation of any children that may have resulted from their ensuing relationship with their abductor. Further, it did not provide any space for the wishes of the women themselves, engendering a double uprooting for those who had made peace with their current situations. The fact that many natal families refused to take back these women did not deter the rehabilitation efforts. Under the leadership of Mridula Sarabhai and well-known social workers such as Sushila Nayyar, Anis Kidwai, Kamlaben Patel, and others, relief workers and the police worked to rescue such women from the other side. The numbers recovered became important to India and Pakistan to indicate the success of the new nation states in 'saving' their women.

Beyond the recovery of abducted women, the Indian state focused specifically on the rehabilitation of women. Special homes were set up for the maintenance of unattached women, and inmates of these homes received vocational training ranging from stenography to midwifery in order to transform them into self-supporting citizens. In some states, rehabilitation policies created specific employment and marriage bureaus to help women refugees. In spite of the limits on rehabilitation policies in general, scholars have noted that in West Bengal, the experiences of refugee women were emancipatory (Chakravartty 2005). They were able to take up jobs to help their families, have relative freedom within the public sphere, and actively participate in the communist movement in the region. In Punjab, too, women were able to break out of traditional restrictions of seclusion and experienced positive impacts in terms of marriage arrangements, access to education, and employment. Moreover, many women who were not refugees themselves but worked towards helping refugees in camps found their initial humanitarian response to Partition victims turn to lifetime commitments and careers in social work.

Nationalizing Citizens: Permits, Passports, and the Indian Constitution

Looming over the Partition's violence and uprooting, and efforts to address them, was the issue of national belonging. While the new border had, for the most part, produced the territorial coordinates of national sovereignties, the continuous movement of people across those borders engendered new questions. Were the people arriving in India from Pakistan Pakistani or Indian? And should the movement of people from India to Pakistan be interpreted as their clear wish for inclusion in Pakistan? Should refugees have the same rights as citizens? The ways in which India and Pakistan addressed these issues of mass displacement, rehabilitation, and regulated movement were crucial to the Partition's legitimacy. The Partition thus became a dialogic process that contributed to the framing of national citizenship.

In the subsequent decades, the refugee crisis in Pakistan and the fissures already in development between East and West Pakistan challenged the development of democratic policies and prevented the formation of a solid foundation for the state. In India, where the refugee crisis was as bad, the state's insistence on protecting its Muslim minorities, even in the face of chronic persecutions and discriminations, went a long way in creating the facade of secularism in post-colonial India. However, in northern India, the Hindu Right, who had been key players in the Partition violence, now did a volte-face to take up the refugee cause and be surrogates who helped the refugees where and when the Indian state failed. In eastern India, West Bengal and Tripura in particular, the communist movement organized the refugees to occupy lands for rehabilitation and to demand rehabilitation from India as their right. India's differential policies on its western and eastern border weakened the forces of centralization in West Bengal, enabling refugee critiques to translate into votes against the Congress government from the 1970s onwards.

Official and public response to the refugee crisis was unable to escape the overarching communal logic that had imbued the political understanding of the Partition. While there were some who spoke in favour of liberal, plural, and secular conceptions of the new states, most implicitly and sometimes explicitly promoted the idea that India was for Hindus and Sikhs and Pakistan would be the abode of Muslims. As refugees arrived in India and Pakistan, they were encouraged to identify themselves as independent citizens of free countries. The victims of violence were called *shahid*s (martyr), and in Pakistan, the Partition was quickly repackaged as a war of liberation. In India, the Hindu and Sikh refugee victims were rewarded with Indian citizenship while Muslim returnees from Pakistan found it increasingly difficult to claim the same.

The common perception that minorities in one country were proxy citizens of the other was strengthened and influenced by India's and Pakistan's attempts to control their mutual borders and by their understanding of the term 'migration'. Recent scholarship has argued that despite the fact that a large number of those displaced by the Partition had temporarily fled their homes and intended to return, both states assumed everyone who moved were 'migrants' (Zamindar 2007). Such an assumption of permanency was a handy tool that helped India and Pakistan to fix people within their territorial boundaries. Moreover, the uprooted were tied to a country because the two states also affixed a certain nationality based on religion. Thus, Muslims were assumed to be Pakistani, and Hindus Indians, irrespective of their territorial location or dislocation.

In 1948, the introduction of 'permits' on the western border contributed directly to such assumptions.

Although aimed at regulating and fixing the identities of all border-crossers between West Pakistan and India, in practice, the use of permits worked towards preventing the flow of Muslims from India and the return of Muslims to India. This meant that Muslims returning to India had to apply for a permit for 'permanent return' to India but would have no subsequent access to rehabilitation, while Hindu and Sikh refugees applied for permits for 'permanent resettlement' that subsequently entitled them to the Indian state's relief and rehabilitation measures. Such practices clearly marked out the Hindus and Sikhs as legitimate 'refugees' while the Muslims as 'migrants' who would not be eligible for state rehabilitation in India. The introduction of the passport and visa systems extended the documentary restrictions on both borders by 1952. The passport quickly evolved from being just a travel document to one that was a marker of citizenship. Both systems, while unpopular with border-crossers, provided Indian authorities with an initial template to test its bureaucratic powers in regulating mobility and ascribing certain rights to those who remained within their borders.

The Indian Constitution and its subsequent Acts on citizenship sought to frame nationality, citizenship, and belonging in multiple ways, but such framing remained ambiguous at best and open to interpretation at various levels. The discussions of the drafting committee, chaired by B. R. Ambedkar, reflect an awareness of the multiple concerns of framing citizenship in such extraordinary times. The framers debated on the provisions for marriages between citizens of India and Pakistan, for residents of seceding areas who might want to retain their Indian citizenship, and the fate of those residents in Burma, Ceylon, Malaya, and Kenya.

By the time the Indian Constitution was adopted, seven Articles (5–11) comprised of issues directly relevant to the question of citizenship. Articles 6, 7, and 9 were specific articulations of citizenship that focused and affected those on the move. In different ways, these three articles and their clauses sought to situate Partition migrants and prevent further movement across the border. One can also clearly see the effort to fix territorial identity with a particular national identity. Article 6 provided citizenship for persons who migrated to India from the territory now included in Pakistan with the condition that either of their parents or grandparents should have been born in India. In addition, it fixed 19 July 1948 as a deadline to be recognized as a migrant eligible for automatic Indian citizenship. Anyone moving after that date would have to be registered as a citizen by a designated authority. It also required that the migrant reside continuously in India after their migration. Consequently, those who travelled back and forth across the border and between divided families became ineligible on the basis of such a domicile clause.

While Article 6 sought to include Partition migrants from Pakistan to India as Indian citizens, Article 7 was designed to exclude those who migrated from India to Pakistan after 1 March 1947. It was very controversial, even at the time of its promulgation, because it provided the rights of citizenship only to those who had returned from Pakistan to India with a permit for resettlement or permanent return. These conditions meant two things—first, Muslims who had temporarily migrated to Pakistan and did not return by 26 January 1950 (the date of the announcement of the Constitution) were automatically deemed to be non-Indians. Second, those who managed to return would have to acquire official documentary proof of their return, which was often difficult to obtain. It was far easier just to cross the border without documents on the basis of a simple permit or, after 1952, on the basis of a Pakistani passport. The last resort became hugely problematic as it went against Article 9, which stated that anyone who voluntarily acquired the citizenship of a foreign state would cease to be a citizen of India. The acquiring of a passport, in this case of Pakistan, was immediate grounds for the loss of Indian citizenship.

The fate of Indians overseas in places such as British East Africa and the issue of their citizenship did not escape the arc of the Partition's communal logic. Thus, an officer at the Indian Commission in Nairobi identified specific Muslims within the overseas Indians as 'constructive evacuees' who, by virtue of demonstrating their attachment to Pakistan, were to be considered in the same category as those Muslim evacuees who had left India for Pakistan (Sutton 2007). Such fantastical assumptions did not see the light of day. However, in their policies towards overseas residents in East Africa, the Indian state aimed to create loyal citizens and assert their authority to bestow citizenship to only those they deemed to be pro-Indian. Such visions of extraterritorial citizenship were untenable and wracked with inherent contradictions, leading the Indian state to formally exclude overseas Indians from citizenship by 1955.

Along with borders, documentary forms of identification, and in their ability to confer citizenship to migrants and refugees, the Indian and Pakistani states remade themselves distinctly into post-colonial nations. Both India and Pakistan prioritized the framing of their respective nation states in the shadow of Partition violence and uprooting. Consequently, their policies towards refugees and minorities were tailored to meet the needs of national security and economic development. As we shall see in the next chapter, such priorities significantly ensured that the Partition did not end in 1947. Its legacies continued to reverberate not only through national politics but also in the lives of individuals and divided families.

4

Legacies, Memories, and Representations

Partition was to be a strategic method of conflict resolution. Instead, it engendered bitter rivalries between India and Pakistan over Kashmir, their mutual borders, and shared water resources. Both nations had to deal with the relief and rehabilitation of refugees and address complex issues of citizenship engendered by Partition migration. The status of specific groups such as the Muhajirs in Pakistan, Biharis in Bangladesh, and Muslims in India contested these states' nation-building efforts as well as their goals of secularism and of framing post-colonial democracies. Such goals were tested anew in 1971, with the creation of Bangladesh and the consequent renewed violence and uprooting, and again in 1984, 1992, and 2002, when riots in India targeted Sikh and Muslim minorities.

In Pakistan, 1947 marked the crystallization of Muslim hopes and the culmination of claims of sovereign nationhood, albeit one that came at a huge human cost. However, such hopes remained unattainable given that the Muslim homeland contained nearly as many Muslim citizens inside its territorial boundaries as there were Muslim non-citizens outside of it. This contradiction was neither acknowledged nor resolved, thus becoming 'one of the principal fault lines in Pakistan's quest for identity that is Islamic as well as national' (Jalal 2014). Further, even though the Muslim minority in British India had its own sovereign state, the experience of the Partition, and complicated negotiations during and after it, had made the new rulers of Pakistan realize their comparatively lesser weight in territorial, demographic, economic, and military terms. This 'sentiment of vulnerability' (Jaffrelot 2015) was useful in framing both official political rhetoric and Pakistan's origin story in oppositional terms, within a narrative that was anti-India and anti-Hindu. Such a negative approach went against the possibilities of a democratic Pakistan, concentrating instead on state-sponsored paranoia of survival in which national security became paramount and 'Hindu India' was framed as the arch enemy (Jalal 2014).

Beyond the national political level, the Partition produced divided families, as people, undecided about their futures and in search of opportunities for economic stability, continued to move back and forth in the decade after 1947. Such movement sometimes went beyond the subcontinent to diverse regions such as South East Asia and North America. Within South Asia, minority and refugee families got caught up in the project of framing new nation states, which often pitted the interests of one against the other. Consequently, they experienced a different kind of partitioning in the subsequent decades. In the aftermath of the Partition, minorities experienced the division within implicit demands to prove their national loyalties, while refugees encountered a long and messy road to assimilation. Both encountered the new states via their strategies to regulate movement, control borders, and demarcate their 'new' citizens. Long after the Partition, disputes over citizenship and border crossings continued to dot the legal and political landscape in both countries. In the end, instead of resolving anything, except marking the departure of the British, the Partition remains an 'unfinished business'.

The Partition's multi-layered experiences continue to inhabit the recollections of individuals and families and are reflected in representations, both at the time and subsequently, in oral histories, literature, film, and music. Memories of home and the sense of belonging and loss jostle with depictions of the trauma of violence and the experience of uprooting in these sources. However, it remains difficult to articulate fully the losses that the Partition entailed, which is perhaps why South Asia as a whole still has not found a way to memorialize the Partition separately from the narrative of Independence.

Legacies

One of the major fault lines created between India and Pakistan at the time of the Partition was over the issue of Kashmir. More than 70 years since the Partition, Kashmir continues to occupy a central position in a long-drawn-out bilateral dispute—each state claiming the former kingdom of Jammu and Kashmir in its entirety. Today, Pakistan controls a slice of Kashmir in the north-west, known as 'Azad Kashmir', while China controls a small part in the north-east, called 'Aksai Chin', and the remains are with India. India and Pakistan have gone to war at least three times in which Kashmir has been the direct or indirect bone of contention. The continuing border conflict and potential of terrorism in Kashmir has allowed both India and Pakistan to increase their military expenditure and turn this picturesque region into the most militarized zone in the world.

Such a metamorphosis began within the processes of decolonization and partition, which directed the approximate 565 princely states formerly under indirect British rule to join either India or Pakistan based on geographical contiguity. The future of the princely states was not adequately addressed and little thought was given to those having large minority populations. Although they all became technically independent on 14 and 15 August with the formal end of British rule, their status as independent entities was not a possibility. Rather, they were to sign a permanent 'Instrument of Accession' after consulting with their subjects and merge with either India or Pakistan (Tan and Kudaisya 2000).

Kashmir, one of the largest princely states, had almost equally contiguous boundaries with both India and Pakistan. Furthermore, although it was ruled by a Hindu maharaja, Hari Singh, Muslims constituted 77 per cent of its population. The challenge here was accentuated as Hari Singh decided to weigh his options and held out on his decision to accede beyond the 15 August deadline. The situation changed dramatically in October when certain Pathan tribesmen invaded Kashmir, and Hari Singh viewed it as a threat to oust him as Kashmir's ruler. He appealed for help to Mountbatten who agreed on the condition that Hari Singh join India. Nehru, the new prime minister of India, sent in troops to drive out the rebel forces. As Hari Singh signed the Instrument of Accession and officially joined India, Pakistan sent in troops into Kashmir, starting the first armed conflict between the two new nations. India managed to quell the rebellion and push the Pakistani troops from all but a small portion of Kashmir.

The accession of Kashmir to India has generated controversy since 1947. Some see it as a result of British and Indian manipulation of a situation that could have been resolved internally. Others question the 'accession' document, suggesting that it is fraudulent. However, what is clear is that both India and Pakistan regarded Kashmir as territorially significant and neither would have entertained the possibility of an independent Kashmir. By the end of 1948, India and Pakistan agreed to a ceasefire imposed by the United Nations, which also advised that a plebiscite to ascertain the will of the Kashmiris be held at a later date. India has refused to conduct such a plebiscite citing the presence of Pakistani forces and irregulars in the region.

The deadlock over Kashmir, the disputed legality of the Instrument of Accession (India regards it final while Pakistan does not), and the yet to happen plebiscite has acerbated India-Pakistan relations in the subsequent years. Moreover, Kashmir has become a significant issue for the Indian state itself as Kashmiris have, in recent decades, begun challenging the increasing militarization of the region under the auspices of the

Indian Army. Issues of both domestic and bilateral ties have resulted not only in national jingoism but also in a race for nuclear capabilities, which culminated in successive nuclear tests in 1998 in Pokhran and Chagtai. The nuclear tests, while confirming the continuation of self-reflexive nationalisms at work even 50 years down the line, were a useful reminder of the entwined fates of these subcontinental nations. As Arundhati Roy put it: 'Though we are separate countries, we share skies, we share winds, we share water.... Any nuclear war against Pakistan will be a war against ourselves' (Roy 1998).

The concern for national security is also echoed in the ways India and Pakistan, and later Bangladesh, have managed and controlled their mutual borders. Since 1947, both nations have clashed with each other in high-level official discussions, petty military skirmishes, and imprisonment over border-crossers, both human and animal. Initially, both the western and eastern boundaries remained porous, allowing people to move temporarily to the other side or return to dispose of their belongings. The introduction of permits and later of the passport system effectively closed the borders to such movement. From the 1950s, seasonal labourers, fishermen in the Arabian Sea and the Bay of Bengal, who had inadvertently drifted into foreign waters, and borderland villagers without documentary proof began to be arrested and imprisoned by India and Pakistan.

Both countries viewed such traditional movement as 'trespassing' (Roy 2016). Such frontier incidents sometimes escalated beyond borders to combine with ongoing concerns over national sovereignty, illegal immigration, and Kashmir.

Recent scholarship suggests that border tensions are also the result of how the new nations view their borders and how those living at the borderlands perceive and encounter the border (Cons 2016). For the new nation states, intent on controlling their newly demarcated boundaries, controlling the refugee flows and being able to grant exit and entry into their territories became sine qua non of the post-Partition nation-building projects. Both India and Pakistan implemented documentary systems of passports, visas, and a plethora of other similar paper identities to allow for legal passage. Thus, border-crossers began to be classified as migrants, refugees, infiltrators, aliens, and foreigners depending on the context of their encounters with the state. The boundary award has now manifested itself through barbed wires, policed check posts, and a documentary regime.

One critical aspect of such concerns about Radcliffe's lines is the demarcation of the border itself as part of the boundary between India and Bangladesh that remains disputed. Radcliffe's boundary award was challenged almost immediately and demands for boundary readjustment—especially with regard to the boundary between India and East Pakistan—were made. The India Pakistan Boundary Disputes Tribunal was formed in 1949 to address and adjudicate such demands. In 1974, India and Bangladesh concluded a land boundary agreement that was to resolve the disputes surrounding enclaves, adverse possessions of land, and the settlement of an un-demarcated land border totalling approximately 4 miles spread over border areas in Assam, West Bengal, and Tripura. The unavailability of accurate maps has exacerbated the problem. More significantly, all three nations continue to restrict public access to any accurate maps on the claims of national security. Such cartographic anxieties are a distinct legacy of the Partition.

While the India–Pakistan border remains closely guarded, a zone for small border skirmishes and the stage for the 'carefully choreographed contempt' at Wagah, the view from the India–East Pakistan (now Bangladesh) border presents a contrast to the national security discourse that saturates political and bureaucratic concerns in India, Pakistan, and Bangladesh. Here, the border really is a borderland, within which lies not only the international border, but also borderland societies that are linked to each other socio-economically and in terms of religion and culture that continue to function as connected units.

The India–Bangladesh borderland citizens use various strategies to prevent the imposition of the post-Partition states from disrupting their lives. For example, the India–East Pakistan border often ran through areas where there was a majority religious group on both sides, which meant that trans-border connections between families continue to be maintained. There is also a thriving cross-border connection between markets and consumers even as both states view such activity as illegal and anti-national. The fact that residents at the borderlands view the movement of labour and goods across the international border as normal and necessary, and that this movement often has the support of local politicians and border officials, has ensured the continuation of a stable border economy. In 2016, India and Bangladesh officially sanctioned a number of border *haat*s (markets) along its mutual border.

The Radcliffe boundary imposed artificial borders over what had been unified natural and ecological landscapes. Such imposition had the most consequences when it came to rivers and water resources. In the case of the Indus River basin, the new borders quickly evolved into disputes over water allocation. As recent studies have shown, control over water resources was framed along national needs that superseded any claims of local communities living in

131

these areas (Bhan 2014; Gilmartin 2015). While the sharing of waters in the Indus basin was resolved after protracted negotiations, the conflict over water in the eastern region is a continuing legacy of the Partition. India and Bangladesh continue to dispute the equitable sharing of water, shifting courses of rivers, controlling hydroelectric power, and related development projects. The problems in the eastern region are compounded by the fact that the Radcliffe line goes through the largest deltaic region in the world that contains the three major river basins of the Ganges, Brahmaputra, and the Meghna rivers. Moreover, 54 of the total 57 rivers flowing in this region are shared and have their headworks located in India but impact those living downstream in Bangladesh.

Such ecological interdependence has been challenged politically since 1951 when India wanted to divert the water of the Ganges to the port of Calcutta to increase its efficiency. When bilateral negotiations between India and Pakistan failed on this matter, India made the unilateral decision in 1961 to build a barrage at Farakka on the Ganges, near the international border, to divert the water in spite of protests from Pakistan. By 1975, the construction on the barrage was completed and, given the positive role India played in Bangladesh's war of independence, it was easy to persuade the new nation to accept the validity of the Farakka barrage. However, it has become clear that the barrage is detrimental to those living downstream and has caused environmental damage; it prevents Bangladeshi farmers from making use of 'green revolution' technologies that require intensive irrigation. India and Bangladesh have failed to come to any agreement over the equitable sharing of their water resources, even as the livelihoods of more than 400 million people depend on the outcome of these negotiations (Tan and Kudaisya 2000).

The legacy of the Partition's boundaries, ensuing migration, and problems of border control continue to complicate understandings of citizenship and belonging. Access to documents and official permissions determine the lines between legal and illegal, between citizens and infiltrators, and between legitimate migration and illegitimate influx. By the 1950s, India's laws did not distinguish between Hindu and Muslim arrivals from Pakistan and viewed them as foreigners and migrants, allowing them to become citizens through legal naturalization. However, the understanding and implementation of such laws, as many court cases indicate, was often not clear-cut. Hindu migrants were often regarded as 'refugees' deserving the benefaction of the Indian state, while Muslim migrants and returnees were increasingly viewed as 'infiltrators' migrating to destabilize the Indian nation.

Such issues have been compounded in the states of Assam and Tripura where many saw post-Partition migrants not as fellow Indians but as Bengalis who were taking over non-Bengali lands (Schendel 2005). These migrants were quickly identified by the Indian state as 'infiltrators' and it proceeded to expel them from 1962 onwards. The mantra of 'infiltration' aims to add fuel to fears of a 'demographic invasion' and is rehearsed periodically by chauvinistic political parties that deliberately fail to distinguish between Bengali-speaking Indian citizens and Bangladeshi illegal immigrants. Thus, recent years have witnessed sustained efforts to oust nearly five million inhabitants who have been identified as 'foreigners' both in terms of language (Bengali) and religion (Muslim).

Assam, a frontier zone during colonial rule, had a long history of encouraging Muslim East Bengali peasant migration to develop its uncultivated regions. The new borders drawn in 1947 did little to stop the flow of people, and, in fact, encouraged the migration of Bengali Hindus. Moreover, Sylhet, Assam's Bengali-speaking predominantly Muslim district, was sectioned out to join East Pakistan through a referendum. Given such a demographic chessboard, tensions between ethnic Assamese and Bengali-speaking settlers were very common during colonial rule. In post-Partition

Assam, such tensions have continued but have changed in terms of demographic content with the migration of Bengali Hindus between 1947 and 1971 and then of Bengali Muslims beyond 1971. The controversies revolving around regional and national citizenship have sought resolution through cut-off dates and more recently through defining citizenship more by blood ties and cultural provenances rather than by territorial residence (Baruah 2001; Roy 2016).

The question of national belonging profoundly affected the Muslims in South Asia after the Partition. For those Muhajirs who migrated to Karachi in the wake of the Partition, rehabilitation and assimilation were difficult given that they were mainly urban, educated, and Urdu-speaking groups now in a region dominated by rural, less-educated, Sindhi speakers. The latter, although welcoming at first, were quickly apprehensive at the influx of refugees who they feared would take over the existing economic and educational opportunities. In the 1980s, the city erupted in sectarian and ethnic violence. Such tensions remain unresolved. On the other side of the subcontinent, the Urdu-speaking Muslims from northern India who had moved to East Pakistan faced similar challenges of linguistic and cultural alienation. They were given the label of 'Bihari' even though many did not come from that state.

These non–Bengali speaking Muslims enjoyed relative high status during the Pakistan phase of 1947–71 but were viewed as traitors during and after the 1971 war. The establishment of Bangladesh complicated matters for the Biharis. Considered representatives of Pakistan, they encountered hostility from the local population and currently reside as stateless minorities in segregated enclaves in Bangladesh (Ghosh 2015).

For those 35 million Muslims who decided to remain in India in 1947, the implications of the Partition framed their minority status. In northern India, Partition violence and migration meant a reduction in numbers and the consequent loss of political privilege and bureaucratic representation for the community. More significantly, in the communally charged atmosphere in the aftermath of the Partition and the creation of Pakistan, Muslims who remained in India faced anti-Muslim bias and accusations of being fifth columnists and agents of Pakistan. In post–Partition India, Muslim political mobilization has had to ensure diverse ways to safeguard their interests and rights, effective electoral participation, and representation amidst questions about national loyalty. Such questions have increased in tempo with the increasing political mobilization of Hindu majoritarian parties, the controversies surrounding the Ramjanmabhoomi-Babri mosque issue, and the Godhra riots in 2002.

Memories and Representations

Krishna Sobti, a refugee from Pakistan at the time of the Partition and a well-known novelist, reputedly once stated that the Partition was difficult to forget but dangerous to remember. She was referring to the difficulty writers had in dealing with the communal violence and hatred, which went against the inheritance of traditions of pluralism and shared human values. Thus, a few such as Saadat Hasan Manto were able to express their rage at the unfolding tragedy of Partition, but for others such as Bhisham Sahni, Bapsi Sidhwa, Intizar Hussain, and Sobti, their reflections could only be penned after 20 to 25 years.

Literary and visual representations are significant in their ability to contest official and communal narratives of the Partition. In their emphasis on essential human values amidst the madness of Partition violence and uprooting, literature allows us to focus on the collective and individual experiences of ordinary men and women and underscore the survival of their moral being in the midst of horror (Bhalla 1999). Moreover, such narratives are able to nuance our understanding of the Partition by calling attention to the ways in which gender, caste, consent, and complicity influenced the Partition's outcomes at the level of the individual.

Although Partition novels have distinct storylines, there are some common themes that bind them in how the division is represented. Such writings generally tend to see the pre-Partition time as one where religious communities shared a common interactive cultural life, where communal antagonism was present but transient. Consequently, fictional writing presents the event of the Partition as sudden, rather than inevitability brought on by ancient communal antagonisms. For example, Krishna Sobti's *Zindiginama* places the story in pre-Partition western Punjab where communal strife was rare and all communities lay claim to the religious and linguistic traditions of the region.

Partition violence is central to such fictional narratives and is often represented as unexpected and horrific. The devastating impact of Partition violence is brought out intimately in the short stories of Saadat Hasan Manto, who was himself displaced from India to Pakistan. Written originally in Urdu, Manto's short stories such as 'Toba Tek Singh', 'Thanda Ghost', 'Khol Do', or 'Parhiya Kalima' brought out the logic-defying suddenness of violence while constantly highlighting the primacy of personal relationships over identities informed by religion. Similarly, Khushwant Singh's *Train to Pakistan* and Bapsi Sidhwa's *Cracking India*, to mention two of the many novels, also challenge the straightjacket understanding of communal categories and emphasize the irrationality of the division.

The ways in which women faced specific forms of violence is the subject of multiple representations. Amrita Pritam's *Pinjar* and Jyotirmoyee Devi's *Epar Ganga Opar Ganga* (The River Churning) critique the existing patriarchal discourses of honour and sexual purity and bring to our attention their work within the violence and repatriation of abducted women during the Partition. Such fictional representations were able to break the silence of sexual violence experienced by women and indicate ways in which their bodies became the ideal sites to represent national, community, and family honour. Feminist scholarship has corroborated these themes and pointed out that the repatriation of abducted and raped women and the refusal of Hindu and Sikh families to accept such women was a double violation of these women (Butalia 2015; Menon and Bhasin 1998; Didur 2006; Mookerjea-Leonard 2017).

The themes of migration, dispossession, and the experience of being refugees in familiar yet unfamiliar lands are best captured in the films of Ritwik Ghatak. Ghatak's *Meghe Dhaka Tara* focused on the refugee experience through the trials and tribulations of a displaced Bengali Hindu family. The female protagonist is a victim not only of Partition displacement but also of the class and patriarchal expectations that continue even in the backdrop of the event. In contrast, M. S. Sathyu's *Garm Hawa* provides the experience of a Muslim shoemaker who refuses to relocate to Pakistan after 1947. The dilemma of staying put as a minority in one's hometown is brought poignantly to the viewers as the family is continuously punished for such a decision through social and economic isolation. Like fiction, such films capture not only the human experience of the Partition but, through the act of collective viewing, also create spaces for the reiteration of collective memory and mourning (Sarkar 2009).

Partition memories are necessarily mediated by nostalgia and loss of a homeland. Such memories are necessary not only to deal with the alienation refugees and the displaced felt in their new situations in refugee camps, but also to restructure their new lives. Recent scholarship analysing such memories of loss has shown how both the idea of the homeland and of an idyllic past is constructed. An analysis of a set of essays by Bengali Hindu refugees published serially in the newspaper *Jugantar* in the 1960s and later compiled in a book titled *Chere Aasha Gram* suggests that the construction of an idyllic pastoral homeland is a necessary foil against the writers' present condition in an alien city. Further, the past is represented as one where Hindus and Muslims interacted in harmony, but the latter appear only as a guest rather than an integral part of that imagined past (Chakrabarty 1996).

Not surprisingly, efforts to collect oral narratives systematically only began in the late 1990s as survivors found it difficult to articulate the experience of uprooting, loss, and violence. Initial efforts began with Urvashi Butalia, Ritu Menon, and Kamala Bhasin who focused on bringing women back into the narrative of the Partition through their own voices. They began with their own families and extended that to interviewing diverse groups of ordinary men and women who experienced the Partition as perpetrators and victims of violence, as social workers, as children, as refugees, and as Hindus, Muslims, and Dalits. Others such as Alok Bhalla have interviewed Partition novelists while Ian Talbot and Darshan Singh Tatla have focused on oral testimonies from those living in Amritsar, which was one of the epicentres of violence in 1947. Efforts by the late Jasodhara Bagchi and Subhoranjan Dasgupta to record the testimonies of women have been an important contrast highlighting the differences in the Bengal experience of the Partition.

Several efforts have been undertaken by grass-roots citizenship organizations in recent years to record the memories of those from the Partition generation. While Andrew Whitehead's *Partition Voices* was one of the pioneers in recording and transcribing these memories, recent efforts include the crowd-sourced digital history project *The 1947 Partition Archive* based out of Berkeley, California, and the *Citizen Archive of Pakistan* in Lahore. In addition, efforts to memorialize the Partition's common experiences across borders are already underway with the establishment of the Partition museum in Amritsar and a temporary exhibition in the Manchester Museum.

These testimonies bring out the human experience of the Partition by contrasting stories of victimhood and resilience, of rupture and renewal, of how men and women remember differently, and contest singular and linear narratives of 1947. Significantly, memories of survivors often focus on the violence and the experience of becoming refugees and such memories rarely separate the politics leading up to 1947 with the consequent violence. Often, violence is explained as necessary to defend community and family interests, describing the Partition as a time of war. Scholars have suggested that such framings not only serve to naturalize notions of fundamental opposition between Hindu, Sikh, and Muslim communities, but also validate particular understandings of the Partition as a narrative of sacrifice for the birth of nation states. Moreover, Partition violence is described in survivor testimonies as an example of temporary insanity, an aberration and extraneous, and interviewees often make a clear distinction between *us* as *victims* and *them* as *perpetrators*. The memory of violence is often dislocated, occurring 'out there', to facilitate the idea that the survivor's neighbourhood or village was an exception, and if there was violence, it was caused by 'outsiders' rather than people of one's own community (Sarkar 2009).

Such 'collective amnesia' (Pandey 2001) in the initial decades has given way to recognition that often those who claimed to be victims were also perpetrators of violence. More significantly, women were often victims of violence from their own family and community members. It is clear that Partition survivors, regardless of their location and status in their reframed life, are uncomfortable talking about violence, especially gendered violence. The humiliation and rape of women were perceived as symbolic triumphs of one community over another, and their suffering inflicted by perpetrators outside and inside their families has long been narrated as stories of heroic sacrifices made in order to save one's community. Similarly, several published interviews of social workers connected with refugee relief and the recovery of abducted women not only problematize state intervention and discourses of relief, but also indicate distinct understandings of community and gender. Memories of violence and the impact of relief workers thus remain intractable in the face of such reframing.

Moreover, the shifting meanings of the Partition with the passage of time ensure that memories of the Partition remain fluid as people recollect and interpret particular events in specific ways. Recent research has also included age as a variable in how Partition memories are mediated. It has drawn attention to the 'invisibility' of children within the Partition narratives because one, neither state advocated for the recovery of children who had been kidnapped or were born as a result of abduction and, two, the recovery of their memories present particular challenges. However, thousands of children experienced the Partition as orphans, or being abandoned, and/or left destitute. They faced violence from members of their own community and sometimes within their own family. Those who had been children during the Partition did not have an arsenal of other experiences like adults or the language to deal with their uprooting, which influenced how they mediated their adult lives and relationships (Butalia 2015; Kumar 2002).

Where do such shifting memories and multiple representations of the Partition leave us in terms of understanding the ways in which they shape the contemporary national experiences in India, Pakistan, and Bangladesh? One way would be to conceptualize the Partition as elastic and understand how apparently disparate historical moments in postcolonial India

144

congeal in popular imagination as 1947. Thus, the histories of communal violence in India during 1984, 1992, and 2002 fold into 1947. The continuing incursions in Kashmir, international border skirmishes, the intermittent riots in Ahmedabad, Delhi, and Bombay, and the jingoistic stance of Hindu nationalism against Muslim minorities in India, all become elements of a simultaneous experience. Similarly, the spectre of the Partition reappeared within the bloody civil war in Pakistan that provided the backdrop for the birth of Bangladesh in 1971. In the case of Bangladesh, the national memory of 1947 has been effectively replaced by 1971.

Another way to think about the representations of the Partition is to think of it as shaping a schizophrenic remembering and forgetting of the memories and legacies of 1947. Thus, at one level, there is a collective amnesia that is heightened at times of bilateral tensions between India and Pakistan and 'we remember by refusing to remember' (Kaul 2001). But the passage of time has also allowed South Asians collectively to take stock of their common sense of loss and experiences of trauma and uprooting and to renew connections across borders.

Even as we differ as to who is to blame and how the transfer of power was handled, most will agree that never before in India's history had so few decided the fate of so many. The key questions to ask today are: How do we move forward and not only carry this history with us but also transcend it? And is such a feat even possible?

For Indians, remembering the Partition means recalling the dark side of Independence, a moment of loss—not only of homelands and families and material things but something more—loss of self and identity. For Pakistanis, this same moment is remembered as a moment of liberation—from British rule and from Hindu majoritarian domination—a phase when identity was gained. As the Partition's first-hand witnesses pass away, both India and Pakistan have subsequent generations who have no direct experience of the traumatic events of 1947. The Partition is just a reality for these generations through its representations and memories. Thus, the important question now is not only that the Partition should be represented but also how we can represent it. The therapeutic space can come from acknowledgement of agency and culpability while remembering the acts of decency, morality, and courage along with the memories of trauma. As post-Partition memory continues within projects such as the Partition Museum in Amritsar or the collaborative creations of artists and authors from India, Pakistan, and Bangladesh, there are also attempts to 're-story' the histories of the Partition. Such attempts continue to belie and challenge the political realities in South Asia. Advocating common regional concerns over political differences and acknowledging the common pre-history of 1947 would be a path towards better regional cooperation and moving forward from the trauma of the Partition.

Bibliography

Introduction: Three Partitions

Bandyopadhyay, Sekhar. 2004. *Caste, Culture and Hegemony: Social Dominance in Colonial Bengal*. Thousand Oaks: SAGE Publications, Incorporated.

Butalia, Urvashi. 1998. *The Other Side of Silence: Voices from the Partition of India*. New Delhi, India: Penguin Books India.

Chakrabarty, Bidyut. 2003. 'An Alternative to Partition: The United Bengal Scheme'. *South Asia: Journal of South Asian Studies*, vol. 26 (2): 193–212.

Chatterji, Joya. 1994. *Bengal Divided: Hindu Communalism and Partition, 1932–1947*. Cambridge: Cambridge University.

Daiya, Kavita. 2008. *Violent Belongings Partition, Gender, and National Culture in Postcolonial India*. Philadelphia, PA: Temple University Press.

Dhulipala, Venkat. 2014. *Creating a New Medina: State Power, Islam, and the Quest for Pakistan in Late Colonial North India*. New Delhi: Cambridge University Press.

Didur, Jill. 2006. *Unsettling Partition: Literature, Gender, Memory.* Toronto: University of Toronto Press.

Feldman, Shelly. 1999. 'Feminist Interruptions: The Silence of East Bengal in the Story of Partition'. *Interventions*, vol. 1 (2): 167–82.

Hardy, P. 1972. *The Muslims of British India.* London: Cambridge University Press.

Hashmi, Taj ul-Islam. 1992. *Pakistan as a Peasant Utopia: The Communalization of Class Politics in East Bengal, 1920–47.* Boulder, CO: Westview Press.

Hirsch, Marianne. 2012. *The Generation of Postmemory: Writing and Visual Culture after the Holocaust.* New York: Columbia University Press.

Jaffrelot, Christophe. 1996. *The Hindu Nationalist Movement in India.* New York: Columbia University Press.

Jalal, Ayesha. 1985. *The Sole Spokesman: Jinnah, the Muslim League, and the Demand for Pakistan.* Cambridge: Cambridge University Press.

———. 1998. 'Exploding Communalism: The Politics of Muslim Identity in South Asia'. In *Nationalism, Democracy and Development: State and Politics in India*, edited by Sugata Bose and Ayesha Jalal. Delhi: Oxford University Press.

Kabir, Ananya Jahanara. 2013. *Partition's Post-Amnesias: 1947, 1971 and Modern South Asia.* New Delhi: Women Unlimited.

Kaur, Ravinder. 2007. *Since 1947: Partition Narratives among Punjabi Migrants of Delhi.* New Delhi: Oxford University Press.

Khan, Yasmin. 2007. *The Great Partition: The Making of India and Pakistan*. New Haven: Yale University Press.

Menon, Ritu and Kamla Bhasin. 1998. *Borders & Boundaries: Women in India's Partition*. New Delhi: Kali for Women.

Mookerjea-Leonard, Debali. 2017. *Literature, Gender, and the Trauma of Partition: The Paradox of Independence*. London: Routledge.

Nair, Neeti. 2011. *Changing Homelands: Hindu Politics and the Partition of India*. Cambridge, Mass.: Harvard University Press.

Pandey, Gyanendra. 2001. *Remembering Partition: Violence, Nationalism and History in India*. Cambridge: Cambridge University Press.

Qasmi, Ali Usman and Megan Eaton Robb. 2017. *Muslims against the Muslim League: Critiques of the Idea of Pakistan*. Cambridge: Cambridge University Press.

Rawat, Ram S. 2001. 'Partition Politics and Achhut Identity: A Study of the Scheduled Castes Federation and Dalit Politics in UP, 1946–48'. In *The Partitions of Memory: The Afterlife of the Division of India*, edited by S. Kaul. New Delhi: Permanent Black.

Roy, Haimanti. 2009. 'A Partition of Contingency? Public Discourse in Bengal, 1946–47'. *Modern Asian Studies*, vol. 43 (6): 1355–84.

———. 2012. *Partitioned Lives: Migrants, Refugees, Citizens in India and Pakistan, 1947–65*. New Delhi: Oxford University Press.

Saint, Tarun K. 2010. *Witnessing Partition: Memory, History, Fiction*. New Delhi: Routledge.

Sen, Uditi. 2014. 'The Myths Refugees Live By: Memory and History in the Making of Bengali Refugee Identity'. *Modern Asian Studies*, vol. 48 (1): 37–76.

Sengupta, Debjani. 2015. *The Partition of Bengal: Fragile Borders and New Identities*. New Delhi: Cambridge University Press.

Shaikh, Farzana. 1989. *Community and Consensus in Islam: Muslim Representation in Colonial India, 1860–1947*. Cambridge: Cambridge University Press.

Singh, Anita Inder. 1987. *The Origins of the Partition of India, 1936–47*. Delhi: Oxford University Press.

Spear, Percival. 1958. *India, Pakistan and the West*. London: Oxford University Press.

Talbot, Ian and Darshan Singh Tatla. 2006. *Amritsar: Voices from between India and Pakistan*. Oxford: Berg.

Virdee, Pippa. 2013. 'Remembering Partition: Women, Oral Histories and the Partition of 1947'. *Oral History*, vol. 41 (2): 49–62.

Zamindar, Vazira Fazila-Yacoobali. 2007. *The Long Partition and the Making of Modern South Asia: Refugees, Boundaries, Histories.* New York: Columbia University Press.

Chapter 1: The Road to Partition

Adcock, C. S. 2010. 'Sacred Cows and Secular History: Cow Protection Debates in Colonial North India'. *Comparative Studies of South Asia, Africa and the Middle East*, vol. 30 (2): 297–311.

Ahmed, Rafiuddin. 1988. *The Bengal Muslims, 1871–1906: A Quest for Identity*. Delhi: Oxford University.

Ali, Muhammad. 1988. 'The Communal Patriot, 1912'. In *Sources of Indian Tradition*, edited by Ainslie Thomas Embree, Stephen N. Hay, and William Theodore De Bary. New York: Columbia University Press.

Bandyopadhyay, Sekhar. 1997. *Caste, Protest and Identity in Colonial India: The Namasudras of Bengal, 1872–1947*. London: Curzon Press.

———. 2004. *Caste, Culture and Hegemony: Social Dominance in Colonial Bengal*. Thousand Oaks: SAGE Publications, Incorporated.

Banerjee, Sikata. 2005. *Make Me a Man! Masculinity, Hinduism, and Nationalism in India*. Albany, NY: State University of New York Press.

Banerjee-Dube, Ishita. 2015. *A History of Modern India*. Delhi: Cambridge University Press.

Bhatia, Varuni. 2017. *Unforgetting Chaitanya Vaishnavism and Cultures of Devotion in Colonial Bengal*. New York: Oxford University Press.

Bose, Sugata and Ayesha Jalal. 2011. *Modern South Asia: History, Culture, Political Economy*. Delhi: Oxford University Press.

Chatterjee, Partha. 1998. *The Present History of West Bengal: Essays in Political Criticism*. New Delhi: Oxford University Press, India.

Chatterji, Joya. 1994. *Bengal Divided: Hindu Communalism and Partition, 1932–1947*. Cambridge: Cambridge University.

Cohn, Bernard S. 1998. *An Anthropologist among the Historians and Other Essays*. Delhi: Oxford University Press.

Freitag, Sandria B. 1992. *Culture and Power in Banaras: Community, Performance, and Environment, 1800–1980*. Berkeley: University of California Press.

Gilmartin, David. 1989. *Empire and Islam: Punjab and the Making of Pakistan*. Delhi: Oxford University Press.

Hasan, Mushirul. 1993. *India's Partition: Process, Strategy and Mobilization*. Oxford: Oxford University Press.

Hashmi, Taj ul-Islam. 1992. *Pakistan as a Peasant Utopia: The Communalization of Class Politics in East Bengal, 1920–47*. Boulder, CO: Westview Press.

Hunter, William Wilson. 1871. *The Annals of Rural Bengal*. London: Smith, Elder and Co.

Jalal, Ayesha. 1985. *The Sole Spokesman: Jinnah, the Muslim League, and the Demand for Pakistan*. Cambridge: Cambridge University Press.

———. 2000. *Self and Sovereignty: Individual and Community in South Asian Islam since 1850*. London: Routledge.

Juergensmeyer, Mark. 1982. *Religion as Social Vision: The Movement against Untouchability in 20th-Century Punjab*. Berkeley: University of California Press.

Lynch, Owen. 1969. *The Politics of Untouchability: Social Mobility and Social Change in a City of India*. New York: Columbia University Press.

Malhotra, Anshu. 2004. *Gender, Caste, and Religious Identities: Restructuring Class in Colonial Punjab*. New Delhi: Oxford University Press.

Metcalf, Barbara Daly. 1982. *Islamic Revival in British India: Deoband, 1860–1900*. New Delhi: Oxford University Press.

Nair, Neeti. 2011. *Changing Homelands: Hindu Politics and the Partition of India*. Cambridge, Mass.: Harvard University Press.

Nehru, Jawaharlal. 1975. *Selected Works of Jawaharlal Nehru*, vol. 7. New Delhi: Orient Longman.

Oberoi, Harjot. 1997. *The Construction of Religious Boundaries: Culture, Identity and Diversity in the Sikh Tradition*. Delhi: Oxford University Press.

Pandey, Gyanendra. 1992. *The Construction of Communalism in Colonial North India*. Delhi: Oxford University Press.

Rao, Anupama. 2009. *The Caste Question: Dalits and the Politics of Modern India*. Berkeley: University of California Press.

Rawat, Ram S. 2001. 'Partition Politics and Achhut Identity: A Study of the Scheduled Castes Federation and Dalit Politics in UP, 1946–48'. In *The Partitions of Memory: The Afterlife of the Division of India*, edited by S. Kaul. New Delhi: Permanent Black.

Roy, Haimanti. 2009. 'A Partition of Contingency? Public Discourse in Bengal, 1946–1947'. *Modern Asian Studies*, vol. 43 (6): 1355–84.

Sarkar, Sumit. 1983. *Modern India, 1885–1947*. Delhi: Macmillan.

Sen, Amartya. 1981. *Poverty and Famines: An Essay on Entitlement and Deprivation*. Oxford: Clarendon Press.

Sengupta, Parna. 2011. *Pedagogy for Religion Missionary Education and the Fashioning of Hindus and Muslims in Bengal.* Berkeley: University of California Press.

Talbot, Ian. 1988. *Provincial Politics and the Pakistan Movement: The Growth of the Muslim League in North-West and North-East India, 1937–1947.* Karachi: Oxford University Press.

———. 1990. *Provincial Politics and the Pakistan Movement: The Growth of the Muslim League in North-West and North-East India 1937–47.* Karachi: Oxford University Press.

———. 2016. *A History of Modern South Asia: Politics, States, Diasporas.* New Haven: Yale University Press.

Chapter 2: A Mottled Dawn

Aiyar, Swarna. 1998. '"August Anarchy": The Partition Massacres in Punjab, 1947'. In *Freedom Trauma Continuities: Northern India and Independence*, edited by D. A. Low and Howard Brasted. New Delhi: SAGE Publications, 15–38.

Bandyopadhyay, Sekhar. 2004. *Caste, Culture and Hegemony: Social Dominance in Colonial Bengal.* Thousand Oaks: SAGE Publications, Incorporated.

Banerjee-Dube, Ishita. 2015. *A History of Modern India.* Delhi: Cambridge University Press.

Bigelow, Anna. 2009. 'Saved by the Saint: Refusing and Reversing Partition in Muslim North India'. *The Journal of Asian Studies*, vol. 68, (2): 435–64.

Brass, Paul R. 2003. 'The Partition of India and Retributive Genocide in the Punjab, 1946–47: Means, Methods, and Purposes 1'. *Journal of Genocide Research*, vol. 5 (1): 71–101.

Butalia, Urvashi. 1998. *The Other Side of Silence: Voices from the Partition of India*. New Delhi, India: Penguin Books India.

Chatterji, Joya. 1999. 'The Fashioning of a Frontier: The Radcliffe Line and Bengal's Border Landscape, 1947–52'. *Modern Asian Studies*, vol. 33(1): 185–242 .

———. 2007. *The Spoils of Partition: Bengal and India, 1947–1967*. Cambridge: Cambridge University Press.

Chester, Lucy P. 2009. *Borders and Conflict in South Asia: The Radcliffe Boundary Commission and the Partition of Punjab*. Manchester: Manchester University Press.

Copeland, Ian. August 1998. 'The Further Shores of Partition: Ethnic Cleansing in Rajasthan 1947'. *Past and Present*, vol. 160: 203–39.

Das, Suranjan. 1991. *Communal Riots in Bengal, 1905–1947*. Delhi: Oxford University Press.

Effendi, M. Y. 2007. *Punjab Cavalry: Evolution, Role, Organisation, and Tactical Doctrine: 11 Cavalry (Frontier Force) 1849–1971*. Karachi: Oxford University Press.

Gilmartin, David. 2015. *Blood and Water: The Indus River Basin in Modern History*. Berkeley: University of California Press.

Kaur, Ravinder. 2007. *Since 1947: Partition Narratives among Punjabi Migrants of Delhi*. New Delhi: Oxford University Press.

Khan, Yasmin. 2007. *The Great Partition: The Making of India and Pakistan*. New Haven: Yale University Press.

Lahiri, Nayanjot. 2012. *Marshalling the Past: Ancient India and Its Modern Histories*. Ranikhet: Permanent Black.

Mansergh, Nicholas, Penderel Moon, David M. Blake, and S. R. Ashton. 1983. *The Transfer of Power 1942–47*. London: HMSO.

Manto, Saadat Hassan. 2008. *Bitter Fruit: The Very Best of Saadat Hasan Manto*. Edited and Translated by Khalid Hasan. New Delhi: Penguin Books.

Mayaram, Shail. 1997. *Resisting Regimes: Myth, Memory, and the Shaping of a Muslim Identity*. Delhi: Oxford University Press.

Menon, Ritu and Kamla Bhasin. 1998. *Borders & Boundaries: Women in India's Partition*. New Delhi: Kali for Women.

Naqvi, T. H. 2008. 'The Politics of Commensuration: The Violence of Partition and the Making of the Pakistani State'. In *Beyond Crisis: A Critical Second Look at Pakistan*, edited by Naveeda Khan. Delhi: Routledge India.

Pandey, Gyanendra. 2001. *Remembering Partition: Violence, Nationalism and History in India*. Cambridge: Cambridge University Press.

Roy, Haimanti. 2012. *Partitioned Lives: Migrants, Refugees, Citizens in India and Pakistan, 1947–65*. New Delhi: Oxford University Press.

Sarkar, Sumit. 1983. *Modern India, 1885–1947*. Delhi: Macmillan.

Schendel, Willem van. 2005. *The Bengal Borderland: Beyond State and Nation in South Asia*. London: Anthem.

Sengupta, Anwesha. 2014. 'Breaking up: Dividing Assets between India and Pakistan in times of Partition'. *The*

Indian Economic and Social History Review, vol. 51 (4): 529–48.

Talbot, Ian and Gurharpal Singh. 2009. *The Partition of India*. Cambridge: Cambridge University Press.

Whitehead, Andrew. 1996. *Oral Archive: A People Partitioned*, Interview with Qurratulain Hyder, Escaping from Dehradun, 1 August, SOAS.

Wilkinson, Steven I. 2015. *Army and Nation: The Military and Indian Democracy since Independence*. Cambridge, MA: Harvard University Press.

Zamindar, Vazira Fazila-Yacoobali. 2007. *The Long Partition and the Making of Modern South Asia: Refugees, Boundaries, Histories.* New York: Columbia University Press.

Chapter 3: Refugees, Citizens, and the Making of the Nation

Ansari, Sarah F. D. 2005. *Life After Partition: Migration, Community and Strife in Sindh; 1947–1962*. Karachi: Oxford University Press.

Bagchi, Jasodhara and Subhoranjan Dasgupta. 2003. *The Trauma and the Triumph: Gender and Partition in Eastern India*. Kolkata, Mumbai: Stree.

Bharadwaj, P., Asim Khwaja, and Atif Mian. 2008. 'The Big March: Migratory Flows after the Partition of India'. *Economic and Political Weekly*, vol. 43, no. 35 (30 August–5 September): 39–49.

Bose Kumar, Pradip. 2000. *Refugees in West Bengal: Institutional Processes and Contested Identities*. Calcutta: Calcutta Research Group.

Butalia, Urvashi. 1998. *The Other Side of Silence: Voices from the Partition of India*. New Delhi: Penguin Books.

Chakravartty, Gargi. 2005. *Coming Out of Partition: Refugee Women of Bengal*. New Delhi: Bluejay Books.

Chatterji, Joya. 2007. *The Spoils of Partition: Bengal and India, 1947–1967*. Cambridge: Cambridge University Press.

Cons, Jason. 2016. *Sensitive Space: Fragmented Territory at the India–Bangladesh Border*. Seattle, Washington: University of Washington Press.

Das, Veena. 1995. *Critical Events: An Anthropological Perspective on Contemporary India*. Delhi: Oxford University Press.

Guha, Ramachandra. 2008. *India after Gandhi: The History of the World's Largest Democracy*. London: Picador.

Kaur, Ravinder. 2007. *Since 1947: Partition Narratives among Punjabi Migrants of Delhi*. New Delhi: Oxford University Press.

Khan, Yasmin. 2007. *The Great Partition: The Making of India and Pakistan*. New Haven: Yale University Press.

Kothari, Rita. 2007. *The Burden of Refuge: The Sindhi Hindus of Gujarat*. Chennai: Orient Longman.

Pandey, Gyanendra. 2001. *Remembering Partition: Violence, Nationalism and History in India*. Cambridge: Cambridge University Press.

Roy, Haimanti. 2016. 'Paper Rights: The Emergence of Documentary Identities in Post-Colonial India, 1950–

67'. *South Asia: Journal of South Asian Studies*, vol. 39 (2): 329–49.

Samaddar, Ranabir (ed.). 1997. *Reflections on Partition in the East*. Calcutta: Calcutta Research Group.

Schendel, Willem van. 2003. 'I Am Not a "Refugee": Rethinking Partition Migration'. *Modern Asian Studies*, vol. 37 (3): 551–84.

———. 2005. *The Bengal Borderland: Beyond State and Nation in South Asia*. London: Anthem.

Sen, Dwaipayan. 2012. 'Caste Politics and Partition in South Asian History'. *History Compass*, vol. 10 (7): 512–22.

Sen, Uditi. 2014. 'The Myths Refugees Live By: Memory and History in the Making of Bengali Refugee Identity'. *Modern Asian Studies*, vol. 48 (1): 37–76.

Sutton, Deborah. 2007. 'Divided and Uncertain Loyalties: Partition, Indian Sovereignty and Contested Citizenship in East Africa, 1948–1955'. *Interventions*, vol. 9 (2): 276–88.

Zamindar, Vazira Fazila-Yacoobali. 2007. *The Long Partition and the Making of Modern South Asia: Refugees, Boundaries, Histories*. New York: Columbia University Press.

Chapter 4: Legacies, Memories, and Representations

Bandyopadhyay, Sekhar. 2012. *Decolonization in South Asia: Meanings of Freedom in Post-Independence West Bengal, 1947–52*. New Delhi: Orient BlackSwan.

Bhalla, Alok. 30 October–5 November 1999. 'Memory, History and Fictional Representations of the Partition'. *Economic and Political Weekly*, vol. 34 (44): 3119–28.

Bhan, Mona. 2014. 'Morality and Martyrdom: Dams, Dharma, and the Cultural Politics of Work in Indian-Occupied Kashmir'. *Biography*, vol. 37, no. 1 (2014): 191–224.

Baruah, Sanjib. 2001. *India against Itself: Assam and the Politics of Nationality*. New Delhi: Oxford University Press.

Butalia, Urvashi. 2015. *Partition: The Long Shadow*. New Delhi: Zubaan.

Chakrabarty, Dipesh. 1996. 'Remembered Villages: Representations of Hindu–Bengali Memories in the Aftermath of the Partition'. *Economic and Political Weekly*, vol. 31 (32): 2143.

Cons, Jason. 2016. *Sensitive Space: Fragmented Territory at the India–Bangladesh Border*. Seattle, Washington: University of Washington Press.

Didur, Jill. 2006. *Unsettling Partition: Literature, Gender, Memory*. Toronto: University of Toronto Press.

Ghosh, Papiya. 2015. *Partition and the South Asian Diaspora: Extending the Subcontinent*. London: Routledge.

Gilmartin, David. 2015. *Blood and Water: The Indus River Basin in Modern History*. Berkeley: University of California Press.

Guha, Ramachandra. 2007. *India after Gandhi: The History of the World's Largest Democracy*. London: Macmillan.

Jaffrelot, Christophe. 2015. *Pakistan Paradox: Instability and Resilience*. Oxford: Oxford University Press.

Jalal, Ayesha. 2014. *The Struggle for Pakistan: A Muslim Homeland and Global Politics*. Cambridge: Belknap Press of Harvard University Press.

Kabir, Ananya Jahanara. 2013. *Partition's Post-Amnesias: 1947, 1971 and Modern South Asia.* New Delhi: Women Unlimited.

Kaul, Suvir. 2001. *The Partitions of Memory: The Afterlife of the Division of India.* Delhi: Permanent Black.

Kumar, Nita. 2002. 'Children and the Partition: History for Citizenship'. In *The Partitions of Memory*, edited by Suvir Kaul. Delhi: Permanent Black.

Menon, Ritu and Kamla Bhasin. 1998. *Borders & Boundaries: Women in India's Partition.* New Delhi: Kali for Women.

Mookerjea-Leonard, Debali. 2017. *Literature, Gender and the Trauma of Partition: The Paradox of Independence.* Abingdon: Routledge.

Pandey, Gyanendra. 2001. *Remembering Partition: Violence, Nationalism and History in India.* Cambridge: Cambridge University Press.

Roy, Anupama. August 1998. *Citizenship in India.* New Delhi: Oxford University Press, 2016.

Roy, Arundhati. 'The End of Imagination'. *Frontline*, p. 13.

Roy, Haimanti. 2016. 'Paper Rights: The Emergence of Documentary Identities in Post-Colonial India, 1950– 67'. *South Asia: Journal of South Asian Studies*, vol. 39 (2): 329–49.

Sarkar, Bhaskar. 2009. *Mourning the Nation: Indian Cinema in the Wake of Partition.* Durham N.C.: Duke University Press.

Schendel, Willem van. 2005. *The Bengal Borderland: Beyond State and Nation in South Asia.* London: Anthem.

Tan, Tai Yong and Gyanesh Kudaisya. 2000. *The Aftermath of Partition in South Asia.* London: Routledge.

Index

About the Author

Haimanti Roy is associate professor of history at the University of Dayton, USA. She obtained her PhD for the University of Cincinnati, Ohio, USA. Roy specializes in the political and social history of colonial and postcolonial South Asia.

Roy's previous publications include a book, *Partitioned Lives: Migrants, Refugees and Citizens in India and Pakistan, 1947–65* (OUP, 2012). She has contributed to journals as well and some of her articles include 'Paper Rights: Emergence of Documentary Identities in Post-Colonial India, 1950–67' (*South Asia: Journal of South Asian Studies*) and 'A Partition of Contingency? Public Discourse in Bengal, 1946–47' (*Modern Asian Studies*).